SPECIAL FORCES
SURVIVAL GUIDE

SPECIAL FORCES
SURVIVAL GUIDE
WILDERNESS SURVIVAL SKILLS
FROM THE WORLD'S MOST ELITE MILITARY UNITS

CHRIS MCNAB

Ulysses Press

First published in the U.S. by
Ulysses Press
P.O. Box 3440
Berkeley CA 94703
www.ulyssespress.com

ISBN 10: 1-56975-672-4
ISBN 13: 978-1-56975-672-0
Library of Congress Control Number: 2008904145

Editorial and design by
Amber Books Ltd
Bradley's Close
74–77 White Lion Street
London N1 9PF
United Kingdom
www.amberbooks.co.uk

Project Editor: Michael Spilling
Interior design: Graham Beehag
Cover design: what!design @ whatweb.com
U.S. Proofreader: Emma Silvers
Illustrations: All © Art-Tech

Printed in Dubai

10 9 8 7 6 5 4 3 2

Distributed by Publishers Group West

DISCLAIMER
Neither the author or the publisher can accept responsibility for any loss, injury, or damage caused as a result of the use of techniques described in this book, nor for any prosecutions or proceedings brought or instigated against any person or body that may result from using these techniques. Any decision to use the information in this book must be made by the reader on his or her own good judgment. This book is sold without warranties or guarantees of any kind, and the author and publisher disclaim any responsibility or liability for personal injury, property damage, or any other loss or damage, however caused, relating to the information this book.

CONTENTS

INTRODUCTION

Survival skills are the bedrock of elite forces training. It is pointless to survive a firefight with the enemy only to die of adverse climatic conditions. Special forces soldiers worldwide are taught a core of survival principles, ranging from the right mental attitude to how to make fire and shelter. As a potential survivor, you must also master these principles and techniques—one unexpected day they might ultimately determine whether you live or die.

The psychological foundation of survival is quite simple: Don't panic. If you suddenly find yourself in a survival emergency, your mind will

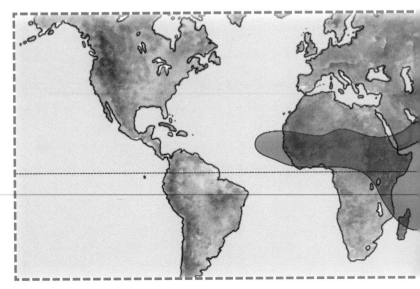

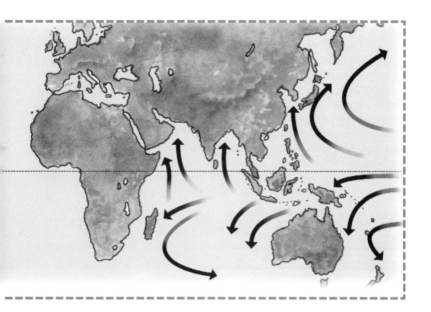

Above: Survival techniques are aided by a working knowledge of the world's climate. The map illustrates the routes that tropical cyclones follow around the world. The Northern Hemisphere is afflicted in July–October, and the Southern in November–April.

Left: The shaded areas illustrate those regions affected by seasonal monsoon conditions. Failure to be aware of the monsoon season can turn a tropical adventure into a survival nightmare. Always confirm the monsoon months before heading into these areas.

flood with disorienting thoughts and feelings. Combat these effects at all costs. Find a place that is sheltered so you can sit down and formulate a blueprint for survival. Good planning and preparation will help you overcome difficulties and dangers and keep you alive. You must be as objective as possible and weigh up all the positive and negative aspects of the situation you are in. Your main priorities are shelter, fire, and water. If you have an abundance of water and also fuel for a fire, i.e. wood, you will also have access to shelter-building materials. If this is the case, you will have all three of your main priorities

• •

Fill out a route card before every outdoor adventure, and make sure you leave a copy with a responsible third party, such as local ranger officers.

ROUTE PLAN

Date: _____ Time: _____ Starting point reference: _____

Weather forecast: _____

Members of party: _____

Description: _____

To (grid reference)	Description (of target)	Direction	Distance	Time (for distance)	Height gain	Time (for height)	Total time	Description (of route and terrain)	Possible alternative route	Escape route

Finishing point reference: _____ Estimated pick-up time: _____

Description: _____ Estimated phone-in time: _____

and should stay where you are in the short term.

To travel or to stay put can be a difficult survival decision. That said, there are powerful reasons to stay put. First, the rescue services may know of your general location and could already be looking for you. Second, by walking you will burn a lot of calories, you will be subject to the elements (which may be harsh, or may become so), you may not be able to set up a permanent and effective signaling system, and you risk literally walking yourself to death. However, if you do decide to travel, you should formulate a plan that includes the following:

- The direction in which you will travel.
- A method of keeping on the course you have determined.
- A schedule of how long you will walk each day.
- A method of signaling.

Remember, you need to allow enough time at the end of each day to establish a camp and a signaling system should an aircraft fly over. If you decide to stay put, your plan must include the following, in order of priority:

- A well-established signaling system.
- A permanent camp or shelter.
- A reliable water source.
- Access to local foodstuffs.

It is critical to establish a signaling system early on, because a spotter aircraft may overfly your position at any time and you must be ready. To this end, it is wise to build your camp near the signaling system. Now you only need survival skills to keep you alive and eventually get back to civilization. Such skills, based directly on those taught to special forces soldiers, will be provided in full in the following chapters.

Research the direction of major land masses on your route. Knowing that a mountain range runs, say, from north to south will give you a constant navigational reference.

Today, because of the explosion in outdoor leisure activities, there is a bewildering variety of clothing available to the backpacker, with a corresponding diversity in quality and price. It is impossible here to give a detailed breakdown of the range of clothing currently available. Nevertheless, some guiding principles can be provided, which will enable you to make a wise choice when selecting outdoor wear.

WHAT TO WEAR

Above all, select the proper clothing for the job. For example, clothing that is suitable for a Sunday afternoon stroll in a temperate climate will not stand up to the severe conditions encountered in the Arctic, tropics, or desert. Undertake detailed research before you embark, and consult experts in adventure sports equipment stores about the right clothing for your trip. This will ensure that you will not find out the hard way that the clothing you purchased is totally unsuitable for the expedition you are currently undertaking.

The layer principle offers the maximum protection and flexibility in all types of climate. The principle is

· ·

Left: Arctic clothing. Note how all the extremities are well protected and maximum warmth is derived from multiple layers. Waterproofing is as critical as warmth.

1

Preparation means having the right tools and clothing to meet any emergency.

Preparation

Comfortable clothing

Uncomfortable clothing can present serious problems over long journeys. Make sure all backpacks are well fitted so they don't restrict circulation to the arms and shoulders, and don't wear so much clothing that you oversweat from exertion.

very simple. Still air is the best form of insulation, and the best way of creating it is to trap it between layers of clothing. The more layers you wear, the greater the insulating effect. Temperature control is very easy. All you do is add or take away layers according to your wants.

Remember, overheating can be as much of a problem as being cold. If you sweat when it's cold, the body chills when you stop sweating, and your sweat-soaked clothing will act as a conductor to draw away body heat into the air. It is important that you prevent this effect. Here are the layers you should wear:

- Next to the skin you should wear thermal underwear.
- Over this should be worn a woolen or wool mixture shirt.
- On top of this will be a woolen or good woven fiber sweater or jacket (woven fiber tends to be better because it is warmer and more windproof).
- Then have a jacket filled with synthetic fiber. Down is not recommended because it tends to lose its insulating properties when it gets wet.
- The final layer must be windproof and waterproof. It should also be made of a "breathable" fabric such as Goretex, which lets sweat evaporate through the fabric into the atmosphere, but

stops rain water from getting in. These last two layers can be combined in a single jacket.

Footwear

For any outdoor activity, it is best to equip yourself with a pair of waterproof boots. The best kind of footwear for general backpacking is walking boots, which have a flexible sole with a deep tread. It is important to look after your boots, and it is always wise to carry a spare pair of laces around with you. Keep the uppers supple and waterproof with a coating of wax or polish, and always check your boots before you use them, looking out for broken seals,

ROYAL MARINES TIPS: CARING FOR YOUR BOOTS

Britain's Royal Marines have two tried-and-tested rules for the care of boots. Stuff wet boots with newspapers and dry them in a warm, airy place, though not in direct heat, which will bake and then crack the leather. In winter, rub silicone or wax over the laces to stop them from freezing when they get wet.

worn-out treads, cracked leather, rotten stitching, and broken fastening hooks. Many backpackers and soldiers wear nylon gaiters over their boots, which helps to keep water out when walking through wet grass and the like.

Socks are another important item of footwear, and most backpackers wear two pairs on their feet for comfort and to prevent blisters. Whether you wear a thin pair and a thick pair, two thin pairs or two thick pairs is up to you, but find a combination that suits you.

Pants

Windproof pants are recommended for outdoor use, but they should also be light and quick-drying. Synthetic/cotton gabardine-type weaves are the best. The better makes of pants are compact, light, and extremely quick to dry, even after being soaked. In addition, they have around five pockets with zippers, making them excellent for carrying items securely. Waterproof leggings can fit over your pants and should have a side zipper (or be wide enough) to allow them to be put on if you are wearing a pair of boots. Be sure they are not tight-fitting. If so, your legs will quickly start to sweat.

Jackets

Your jacket forms your outer shell. It must be windproof and waterproof. The jacket should have a deep hood that can accommodate a hat, come up to cover the lower part of the face, and it should have a wire stiffener. (Hood drawstrings with cord locks are better than the tying variety, especially if you are wearing gloves.)

The sleeves should cover the hands and the jacket should have wrist fasteners. The jacket should also be big enough to accommodate several layers of clothing and enable the flow of air in warm weather. The number of pockets is a personal choice, but you should select a jacket that has at least two on the outside with waterproof flaps and one on the inside for holding a map. The jacket should be knee-length and also have drawcords at the waist and hem.

Color is a matter of choice. Some people prefer the more military-looking types in olive green or camouflage. However, while it may be more pleasing to the eye to wear a color that blends into the surroundings, remember that it will be more difficult for rescue patrols to see you in an emergency. Bright colors, on the other hand, stick out and draw attention to yourself— excellent for a survival situation.

Gloves

There are many woolen and ski gloves available, but mittens are better for heat retention. They can be very awkward if you want to use your fingers, though, so wear a thin pair of gloves under your mittens.

Warm-weather clothing

In hot climates, keep as much of your body as possible covered with light clothing. Always wear eye and head protection.

Headgear

It is estimated that between 40 and 50 percent of heat loss from the body in some conditions can occur through the head. Therefore it is important to wear something on the head (headgear can also provide protection from the heat in hot weather). Any sort of woolen hat or balaclava will help prevent heat loss, though these are not, of course, waterproof.

WHAT TO CARRY

In the fight for survival, a few key items can mean the difference between life and death. All soldiers and travelers should therefore anticipate any life-threatening situations they may face and carry equipment that will help overcome them. The simple rule is: Do not carry useless weight. You want only those things that will serve, not hinder, you.

The survival tin

The survival tin can be one of your most useful stores of equipment. If you always have the items listed below handy, your chances of survival, regardless of the terrain, will be greatly enhanced. These items are not expensive or difficult to operate, and they can fit into an ordinary tobacco tin. Get used to carrying the tin around with you at all times, and regularly check its contents for deterioration, especially the matches and tablets. Pack the contents with cotton balls or cotton wool—it stops annoying rattling and can be used for making fire.

Your survival tin should include the following items: matches, but use only when other improvised fire-making methods fail; candle, both as a light source and because it is useful

U.S. AIR FORCE TIPS: GENERAL CARE OF CLOTHING— THE "COLDER" PRINCIPLE

USAF pilots learn this simple acronym for remembering the principles of survival clothing, designed for when they are stranded in hostile terrain with only their jumpsuits for protection.

C Keep clothing clean.
O Avoid overheating.
L Wear clothing loose and in layers.
D Keep clothing dry.
E Examine clothing for defects in wear.
R Keep clothing repaired.

Survival tin: contents

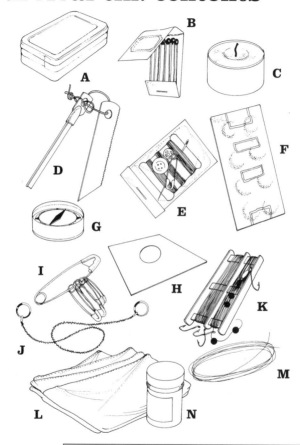

A: tin	H: signaling mirror
B: matches	I: safety pins
C: candle	J: wire saw
D: flint/striker	K: fishing line
E: sewing kit	L: plastic bags
F: water purification tablets	M: snare wire
G: compass	N: potassium permanganate

Guides and maps

Study geologically detailed maps of any area to which you intend to travel. Use guidebooks to discover about regional flora and fauna, and research the cultural practices of local people.

for starting a fire (tallow wax can be eaten in an emergency); flint, specifically a processed flint with a saw striker—this combination can make hundreds of fires, and will carry on working long after your matches have been used up; sewing kit, useful for repairing clothes and other materials; water purification tablets, useful when water supplies are suspect and you do not have boiling facilities; compass (a small button, liquid-filled compass is the best, but check regularly for leaks); a small

Field rations

Rations should be designed around what will satisfy the balanced nutritional and energy requirements of your survival. Here are some examples of durable foods that together serve both short- and long-term energy needs.

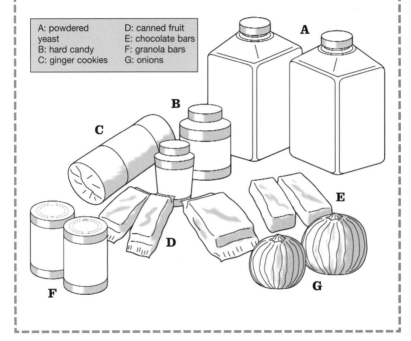

A: powdered yeast
B: hard candy
C: ginger cookies
D: canned fruit
E: chocolate bars
F: granola bars
G: onions

mirror for light signaling; safety pins, useful for securing items of clothing and for the manufacture of improvised fishing lines; fish hooks and line—the fishing kit should also include split lead weights, and have as much line as possible, which can

also be used to catch birds; a wire saw, which can cut even large trees (cover it in a film of grease to protect against rust); large plastic bag, used to carry water and also for making a solar still and vegetation bag; potassium permanganate, which has many uses—for example, it can make an antiseptic and treat fungal diseases when added to water; snare wire (brass wire is the best, and can be used repeatedly for animal traps).

Survival bag

It is also useful to make up another, larger survival kit, one that will fit into a small-sized bag and which can be carried in your car or with you on trips. As with the survival tin, get used to always having it with you, and make sure you regularly check its contents for any signs of deterioration. The items you should carry in the bag are: sewing kit, pliers with wire cutter, dental floss (for sewing), pocketknife, ring saw, snow shovel, signal cloth (at least

First-aid kit

A good first-aid kit should include items to treat wounds, limit or treat infections, safely reduce pain, and aid in delivering life-saving techniques. Make sure you are properly trained in how to give antibiotics and painkillers, if you carry them.

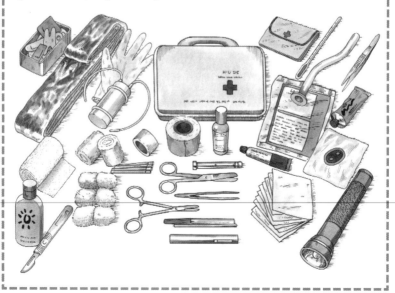

Essentials

Pack essential, often-used items such as flashlights, maps, compasses, knives, first-aid kits, and fire-starting equipment in easily accessible pouches, pockets, and bags. Make sure any survival bags you use are completely waterproof and free from tears.

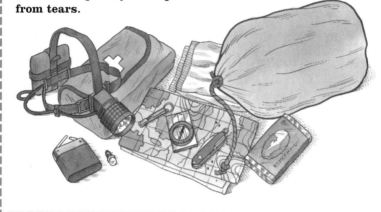

3 feet by 3 feet/1 meter by 1 meter), fishing hooks, flies, weights and line, three large safety pins, 150 feet (45m) of nylon line, gaff hook, multivitamins, protein tablets, large chocolate bar, dried eggs, dried milk, file, cutlery set, three space blankets, compass, signal mirror, four candles, microlite flashlight with extra batteries and bulbs, fire starter, windproof and waterproof matches, butane lighter, flint, insect repellent, 12 snares, spool of snare wire, can opener, plastic cup, water purification tablets, sling shot and ammunition, knife sharpener, whistle, soap, two orange smoke signals, 225 feet (67m) of nylon twine, 225 feet (67m) of nylon cord, one pair of work gloves, a mess tin, and a mousetrap.

Tents and portable shelters

A portable shelter is an essential item of any outdoors kit. As with the clothing, there is a vast range to choose from, ranging from ultra-lightweight mountain and arctic models to inexpensive types for summer weather. To select a tent

Mess pack

A basic mess pack provides some simple nutrition plus the means for keeping clean in the wilderness.

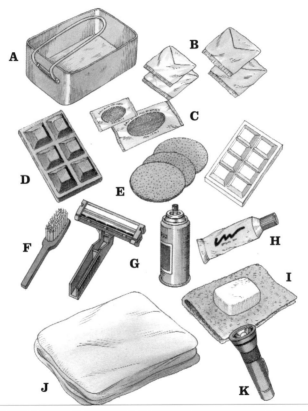

A: mess tin	D: chocolate	H: toothpaste
B: tea and coffee pouches	E: cookies	I: soap and facecloth
C: milk and sugar pouches	F: toothbrush	J: fluorescent survival bag
	G: razor and shaving foam	K: flashlight

Pocket fuel

The foods below are light to carry but together provide a good mix of sugars, fats, carbohydrates, and vitamins. Top to bottom, left to right: hard candy; trail mix; granola; dried fruit; oats; rice; lentils; kidney beans; chocolate.

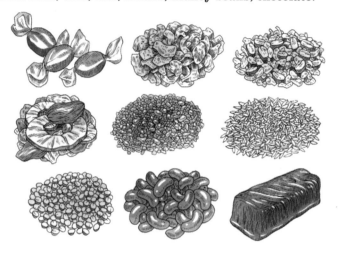

tailored to your specific needs, look at brochures and magazines, and go to tent displays or to camping retailers that display them on the premises. Most modern tents are not heavy, so unless weight is your overriding priority, go for a tent that has plenty of internal space.

A bivouac bag (or bivi-bag) is a portable shelter that has gained popularity in recent years. This is simply a waterproof overall for a sleeping bag, and some have hoops that convert them into a low-profile, one-man tunnel tent. You can't really cook inside a bivi-bag, but it is windproof, waterproof, and very lightweight—as little as 19 ounces (0.54kg). In addition, because they are "breathable," condensation will not collect inside them, so your sleeping bag will remain dry.

Geodesic (dome-shaped) tents offer plenty of internal space. Indeed, many have enough space between the fly sheet and the inner tent to enable you to cook or store equipment. If they have two entrances, you can do both, which keeps the inner tent free of clutter.

Cooking equipment

There are many commercial cooking stoves to choose from, but there are two important rules you should bear in mind when making your selection:

- Keep it as lightweight as possible.
- Do not buy a stove that has a lot of extra parts. They can snap off easily and become lost when being used in the outdoors.

The choice of fuels for stoves is also wide: butane/propane, paraffin, methylated spirit, and gasoline. However, if you intend to cook inside a confined space, keep the following information in mind:

- Paraffin stoves should be refueled only when they are cold. When they are burning, ventilate the tent to prevent the buildup of toxic gases.
- Gas can freeze in low temperatures.
- Leaded gasoline in stoves is a danger to health when burned inside a tent; always use unleaded gasoline.
- Hexamine blocks must never be burned inside a tent.

Regarding cookware, there is a large choice available, ranging from the ubiquitous aluminum mess tin to stainless steel cooking sets. The latter usually come in sets of four or five items that fit inside one another to form

Knives

In the wild, it's a good idea to carry two knives—a strong, high-quality sheath knife, plus a folding pocketknife should your main blade be lost.

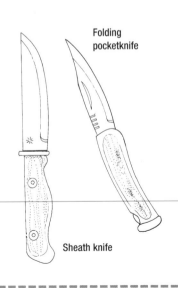

Folding pocketknife

Sheath knife

a very compact set—excellent for space saving. However, before you rush out and buy a set, ask yourself if you really need this much cookware. For crockery, plastic is probably the best—it is lightweight and will not rust.

Knives

A knife is extremely important in a survival situation. It can be used for many things, such as skinning animals, preparing fruits and vegetables, and cutting trees. Always

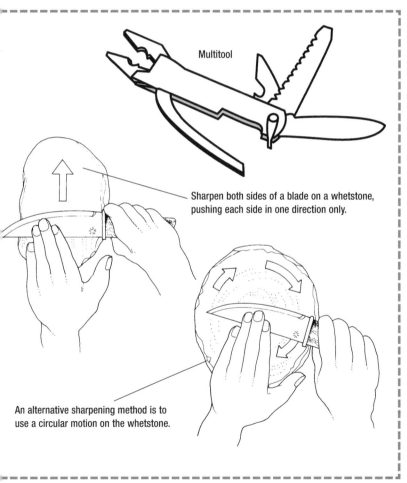

Multitool

Sharpen both sides of a blade on a whetstone, pushing each side in one direction only.

An alternative sharpening method is to use a circular motion on the whetstone.

keep your knife clean and sharp and make sure it is securely fastened when you are traveling. (Never throw your knife into trees or into the ground; you could damage or lose it.) There are many knives to choose from, but it is best to have one that has a unitary blade and tang and a wooden or horn handle.

Backpacks

There are many backpacks available to the adventurer, ranging from small 4.4-gallon (20-liter) capacity packs to the large 22-gallon (100-liter) capacity backpacks. However, remember to get one that suits your needs, and don't get one that is unnecessarily large for your purposes. Here are some of the things you should look for when buying a backpack:

• Side pockets, useful for carrying those items to which you need easy access.

SPECIAL FORCES TIPS: LOAD PACKING AND CARRYING

Special forces troops avoid back injuries by observing the following rules for load carrying.

• Keep the load as light as possible. Maximum load per person should be one-quarter of his weight. Resist the temptation to fill your pack with unnecessary bulk.

• Keep the load as high as possible. Adjust packs to keep the load close to the back, but DO NOT restrict circulation to the arms.

• Inside packs, arrange items to give a balanced loading. Corners of cans, footwear, and hard objects must be kept away from the back.

• Put everything in plastic bags (no pack is 100 percent waterproof), and put the least frequently needed items at the bottom of the pack.

• Put the stove and fuel in side pockets, and anything else that will be needed when walking. This will make having to take off the pack unnecessary.

• During short stops, do not take off the pack; rather, use it as a backrest when lying down, or sit up with it supported on a rock or log.

• Side compression packs, useful for evenly distributing the load inside the pack and also for carrying additional equipment.

• Base compartment, allows the load in the pack to be divided for

Backpack

Your backpack should be lightweight, waterproof, and comfortable to wear over long distances. Pack the most frequently used items in the top and the side pouches, and put wet or dirty items in the base compartment (ideally wrapped in a sturdy plastic bag).

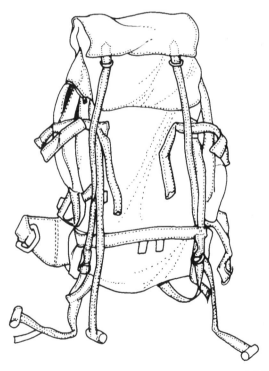

Horseshoe pack

The horseshoe pack is an expedient method of carrying supplies in the absence of a professional backpack. Simply wrap up all the items for carrying in a large sheet (preferably of waterproof material) and tie off the ends, then use further cords to divide the pack into thirds (these stop the contents from sliding around). Finally, sling the pack over one shoulder and tie the two ends at the opposite hip.

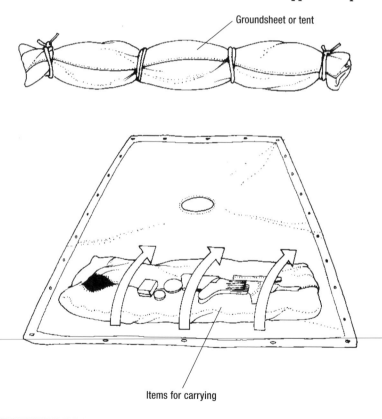

Groundsheet or tent

Items for carrying

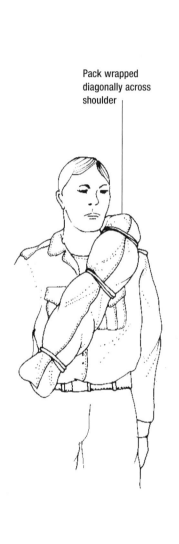

Pack wrapped
diagonally across
shoulder

weight distribution purposes and ease of access.
- Extendable lids can vary backpack capacity.
- Double stitching, binding, and bar tacks increase both strength and protection.

At the other end of the backpack scale is the horseshoe pack, which can be used to carry items comfortably over long distances. The procedure for making one is as follows: lay a square-shaped sheet of material 5 feet by 5 feet (1.5m by 1.5m) on the ground; place all items on one side of the material; then roll the material with the items to the opposite edge. Tie each end and have at least two evenly spaced ties around the roll. Then bring both ends together and secure. What you now have is a compact and comfortable pack, which you can change from shoulder to shoulder if required.

Sleeping bags

Good sleeping bags are filled with down, the best insulating material. In wet conditions, you will need a waterproof cover for a down-filled bag. If you know you will be sleeping in wet conditions, get a bag filled with lightweight synthetic stuffing. You could opt for a light (but expensive) all-weather sleeping bag. This is a sleeping bag, a fleece liner, and a bivi-bag all in one.

O f all the elements of survival, water is the most important. In a survival situation, it is possible for a person to live without food for weeks in certain conditions. Without water, however, death will come within days. Therefore, finding water is the number one priority for all survivors.

REQUIREMENTS

In a temperate climate, a person needs to drink at least half a gallon (2.5 liters) of water a day. Water requirements are increased in some circumstances or if you suffer any of the following:

- Heat exposure: when exposed to high temperatures, you can lose more than three-quarters of a gallon (4 liters) of water per hour by sweating.
- Exercise: increased water loss through the lungs is a result of a higher respiration rate and increased perspiration, both the consequences of exercise.
- Cold exposure: the amount of water vapor in the air decreases and the temperature falls in the cold. Breathing in cold air increases water loss through evaporation from the lungs.

••••••••••••••••••••••••••••••••

Left: Water needs to be collected, filtered, and purified to make it safe for drinking.

2

Even in freezing climates, finding water can be your top survival priority.

Water

Water storage

Water storage vessels range from small hip canteens through to large water bags.

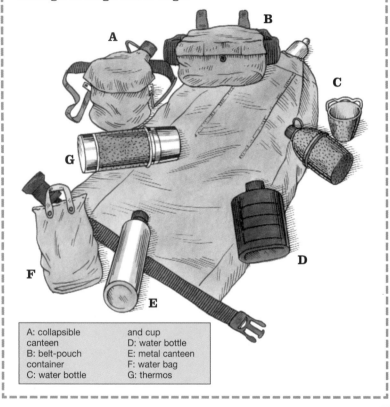

A: collapsible canteen
B: belt-pouch container
C: water bottle
and cup
D: water bottle
E: metal canteen
F: water bag
G: thermos

- High altitude exposure: there is a marked increase in the loss of water through breathing in colder air, and fluid loss is further increased by the efforts required to breathe at higher altitudes.

- Burns: burning destroys the outermost layers of the skin, which acts as a barrier to water diffusion, and water loss from the body increases dramatically as a result.

• Illness: water loss is increased if the victim suffers from vomiting or diarrhea.

Dehydration itself is a potentially life-threatening condition. The symptoms are a loss of appetite, lethargy, impatience, doziness, emotional instability, slurred speech, and a failure to be mentally coherent. The treatment is straightforward: replace lost fluids by drinking water. Multiple water bottles should therefore be an essential item of any backpacker's kit.

Minimizing water loss
Any survivor should take measures to reduce water loss. All physical activity should be reduced to a minimum. Perform all tasks slowly to lessen the expenditure of energy,

U.S. AIR FORCE TIPS: IDENTIFYING CONTAMINATED WATER

Do not waste time in a survival situation by trying to purify contaminated water. Follow U.S. Air Force training and avoid the following water sources:
• Those with strong odors, foam, or bubbles in the water.
• Those with discoloration of the water.
• Those that lack healthy green plants around water sources.

Poisonous water

If possible, avoid collecting water from stagnant ponds, often indicated by surface foam and dense growths of cattails and bullrushes.

Rain trap

Large, curved leaves can be formed into gutters to catch and divert rainfall into a container. Wide and glassy-surfaced tropical leaves are particularly good for this purpose.

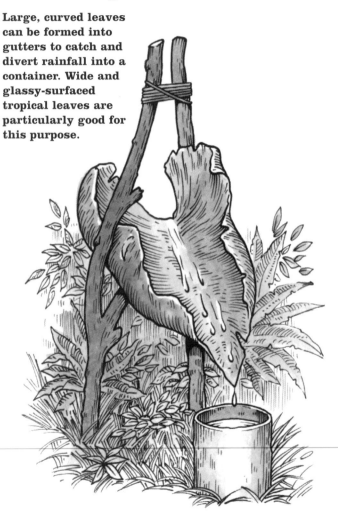

and have regular rest periods. In hot climates, carry out essential activities at night or during the cooler parts of the day. In addition, wear clothing to reduce fluid loss. There is always a temptation to take off clothing in hot climates. Don't! Perspiration in clothing cools the air trapped between the clothing and the skin, resulting in a decrease in the overall activity of the sweat glands and thus a reduction in water loss. Wear light-colored clothing in hot weather because it reflects the sun's rays and keeps any increase in body temperature to a minimum.

Rain collection

A large rain-collection device such as this one, which uses a suspended waterproof groundsheet and stone weights to divert the flow of water, will collect many gallons of fresh water in just a few minutes during heavy rainfall. Ensure that you have containers at the ready when rain approaches.

SAS TIPS:
MINIMIZING WATER LOSS

The soldiers of the British Special Air Service, who often have to survive behind enemy lines with few supplies, know how to cut down on fluid loss.
- Rest as much as possible.
- Avoid smoking and drinking alcohol; the latter uses fluids from the vital organs to break it down, and smoking increases thirst.
- Stay in the shade.
- Avoid lying on hot or heated ground and surfaces.
- Eat as little as possible: the body uses fluids to break down food; this can increase dehydration.
- Do not talk, and breathe through the nose not the mouth.

FINDING WATER

More techniques for finding water are given in Chapter 7, but the following are some essential rules for tracking down water in any terrain. Indicators of water sources include the following:

- Swarming insects—look for bees and columns of ants.
- Birds—may gather around water, though note that water birds can travel for long distances without water and their presence may not indicate a water source. Birds of prey obtain liquids from their kills and are not indicators of a source of water.
- An abundance of vegetation of many varieties. This often indicates that the plants are

Finding water

When exploring dried-up riverbeds for water, dig down at the outer bends of the river. Along with shaded, rocky places, these are usually the last locations from which the surface water evaporated, and therefore the most likely locations to have undergound water.

Sediment hole

By digging a hole into damp earth, water will steadily seep into the hole from other locations.
The collected water will need a lot of filtering.

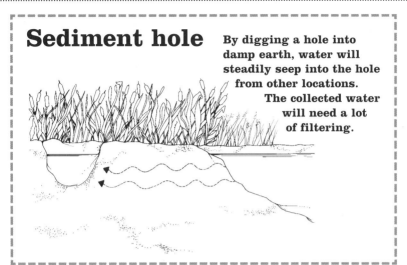

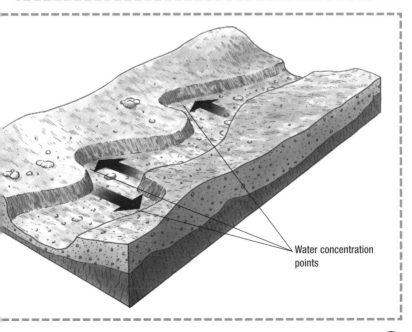

Water concentration points

37

Collecting dew

Dew is best collected from expanses of grassland. Use water-absorbent material such as cotton and rub it over the dew-covered grass.

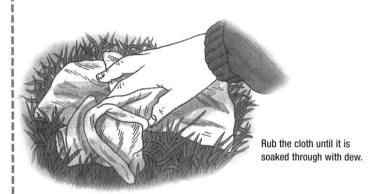

Rub the cloth until it is soaked through with dew.

Wring the dew into a container, such as a bucket.

Water soak

The cloth wrapped around the tree becomes soaked by rainwater, which eventually drips out into the container placed below. This water is usually safe to drink.

drinking from water that is near the surface.

- Animals—grazing animals need water at dusk and dawn, though meat-eaters get liquids from their prey and their presence may not indicate a local water source.
- Large clumps of lush grass may indicate a source of water.
- Animal tracks—these often lead to water.
- Springs and seepages in rocky terrain—limestone and lava rocks will have more and larger springs than other rocks.
Lava rocks contain millions of bubble holes, through which water may seep.

- Cracks in rock with bird dung outside—may indicate a water source that can be reached by a straw.
- Valley floors—dig along their sloping sides to find water.

Remember to collect as much rainwater as you possibly can whenever you have a downpour. A simple method of gathering rainwater is to wrap a cloth around a slanted tree and ensure the bottom of the cloth drips into a container. You should also leave out pots and containers to catch the water, or even dig a pit lined with plastic for large-scale rain gathering.

Water reservoir

This water reservoir consists of a large pit lined with a waterproof sheet. However, attempt to dig such a feature only if you already have plenty of food, water, and energy to sustain the effort, and if you are not planning to move soon.

Filtering through a sock

A sock filter is good for filtering out large particles of dirt or vegetation from a sample of water. Tighter-knit cotton socks tend to be more effective.

METHODS OF PRODUCING WATER

The solar still is an excellent way of procuring small but potentially life-saving quantities of water. Dig a hole 3 feet (90cm) across and 2 feet (60cm) deep, and also dig a sump in the middle of the hole and put a container in it. Then place a plastic sheet over the hole and secure it with sand, dirt, or rocks. Place a rock in the center of the sheet. The sun raises the overall temperature of the air and soil in the hole to produce vapor. Water then condenses on the underside of the plastic sheet and runs down into the container.

The solar still can also be used to distill pure water from contaminated water or seawater. Dig a small trench around 10 inches (25cm) from the still and pour the polluted water or seawater into it. The soil will filter it as it is drawn into the still.

A vegetation bag works on a similar principle to the solar still.

Solar still

The important point when constructing a solar still is not to leave any gaps around the edge of the plastic from where the water vapor inside the still can escape.

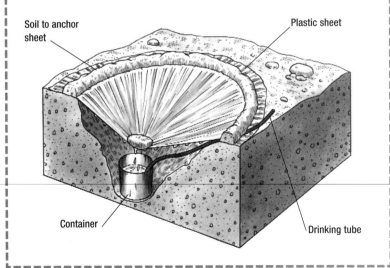

Soil to anchor sheet

Plastic sheet

Container

Drinking tube

Transpiration bag

Note how the vegetation does not touch the sides of the transpiration bag here. If it does, the foliage can sometimes reabsorb the condensation forming on the plastic.

Cut foliage from trees or herbaceous plants and seal it in a large, clear plastic bag. Lay the bag in the sun. The heat will extract the fluids contained in the foliage. Alternatively, place a large plastic bag over the living limb of a tree or large shrub. Seal the bag opening at the branch. Tie the limb or weigh it down so the water will flow to the corner of the bag. Make sure any plastic bag you use is free of holes, which will let water vapor escape. A new branch should be used each day, and the water collected at the end of the day.

Remember, all water needs to be clean before drinking. Filtration does not purify water, it only removes the solid particles. Make a porous bag (from a cotton T-shirt, for example) and fill it with alternate layers of sand and stones, then filter the water by pouring it through. Alternatively, stretch layers of material across a tripod and fill each layer with grass, sand, and charcoal (see illustration). All water taken from survival sources should be purified before drinking to kill germs (see box, page 44).

Saltwater still

A saltwater still involves boiling saltwater in a container covered with a thick cloth. The steam soaks the cloth, and the trapped water can then be wrung out into a separate container. The salt is left behind in the boiling pot.

U.S. SPECIAL FORCES TIPS: METHODS OF PURIFYING WATER

U.S. Green Berets are taught these three simple ways of purifying water at the John F. Kennedy Special Warfare Center and School.

- Use water purification tablets (one in clear water, two in cloudy).
- Five drops of two percent iodine in a container of clear water; 10 drops in cloudy or cold water (let it stand 30 minutes before drinking).
- Boil water for 10 minutes.

Water filter

The contrasting layers of this water filter will each strip out particles of debris from the water, leaving it clean enough to be boiled for purification.

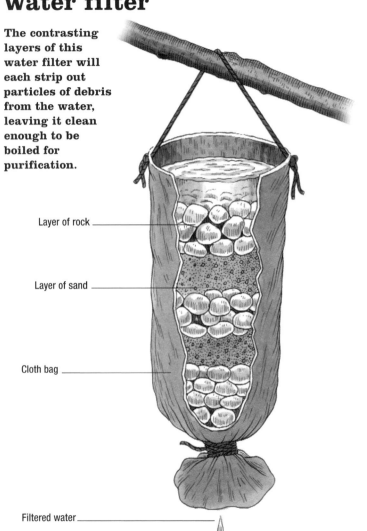

Layer of rock

Layer of sand

Cloth bag

Filtered water

T he average energy requirements are up to 3,000 calories a day for a man and up to 2,000 calories for a woman. However, in a survival situation, where you undertake more strenuous activity, you will need more: 3–5,000 calories a day in warm weather and 4–6,000 calories a day in cold climates.

You must try to eat a balanced diet to keep your body and mind working properly. This means ensuring you eat each of the major food groups on a daily basis. These groups are categorized as follows:

Protein: essential for growth and repair of tissue. Also an energy source when inadequate amounts of carbohydrates and fats are present. Protein is found in cheese, milk, cereal grains, fish, meat, and poultry.
Carbohydrates: very simple molecules that are easily digested. They are the body's main source of energy. For the survivor, they should constitute up to half of the daily caloric intake. Carbohydrates can be obtained from fruit, vegetables, chocolate, milk, and cereals.
Fats: the most concentrated energy source. Fats can be obtained from

••••••••••••••••••••••••••••••

Left: The accessibility of food depends upon many factors, such as terrain, local flora and fauna, time of the year, and also your skills as a hunter and forager.

3

A survival diet is about eating everything you need to supply critical energy and nutrition.

Food

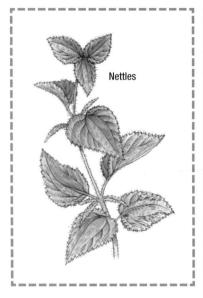

Nettles

butter, cheese, oils, nuts, egg yolks, margarine, and animal fats.

Vitamins: regulate the body's vital functions. There are many kinds, but most can be obtained by maintaining a balanced diet.

Minerals: regulate the body's functions and form vital constituents of teeth and bones. Like vitamins, a well balanced diet should ensure an adequate supply of minerals.

FOOD FROM PLANTS

Thousands of edible plants are found throughout the world. When selecting unknown plants to eat, you MUST carry out the Universal Edibility Test to check they are safe to eat (see box opposite). Many plants have one or

Dig up roots

Sharpen the end of a long, strong branch into a flat, "screwdriver"-like profile.

Dig down around the root, loosening the soil and using the stick to lever the root out.

more edible parts, so it is important to test all parts of the plant.

Edible parts of plants

Tubers, usually found below ground, are rich in starch and should be roasted or boiled. Plants with edible tubers include arrowhead, tara, yam, cat's-tail chufa, and sweet potato.

U.S. ARMY TIPS: UNIVERSAL EDIBILITY TEST

Use this simple U.S. Army test for establishing whether a plant is safe to eat. Note: It CANNOT be applied to fungi.

- Test only one part of the plant at a time.
- Break plant into its base constituents: leaves, stem, roots, etc.
- Smell the plant for strong or acid odors.
- Do not eat for eight hours before starting the test.
- During this period, put a sample of the plant on the inside of your elbow or wrist; 15 minutes is enough time to allow for a reaction.
- During the test period, take nothing orally except pure water and the plant to be tested.
- Select a small portion of the component.
- Before putting it in your mouth, put the plant piece on the outer surface of the lip to test for burning or itching.
- If after three minutes there is no reaction, place it on your tongue; hold for 15 minutes.
- If there is no reaction, chew a piece thoroughly and hold it in your mouth for 15 minutes. DO NOT SWALLOW.
- If there is no irritation whatsoever during this time, swallow the food.
- Wait eight hours. If any ill effects occur, induce vomiting and drink plenty of water.
- If no bad effects occur, eat half a cup of the same plant prepared the same way. Wait another eight hours; if no ill effects are suffered, the plant as prepared is safe to eat.

Roots and rootstalks are also good sources of starch. Plants with edible rootstalks include baobab, goa bean, water plantain, bracken, reindeer moss, cow parsnip, wild calla, rock tripe, canna lily, cattail, chicory, horseradish, tree fern, lotus lily, Angelica, and water lily. Note that some bulbs can be poisonous—e.g. death camas—but others are edible—e.g. wild lily, wild tulip, wild onion, blue camas, and tiger lily.

Edible shoots grow in much the same way as asparagus. Many can

Edible plants

The plants below are common in temperate zones during the summer months, and provide a good spectrum of vitamins, fats, protein, and sugars.

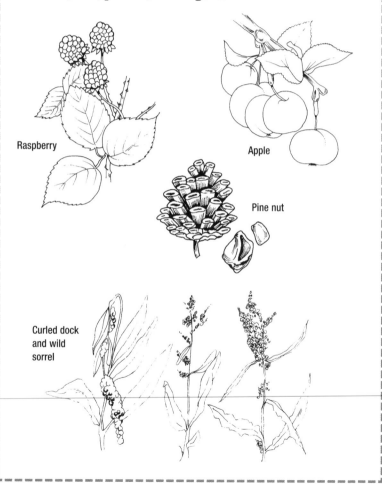

Raspberry

Apple

Pine nut

Curled dock and wild sorrel

be eaten raw, but they are better boiled. Edible shoots include purslane, reindeer moss, bamboo, fishtail palm, goa bean, bracken, rattan, wild rhubarb, cattail, sago palm, rock tripe, papaya, sugar cane, and lotus lily.

Plants with edible leaves are perhaps the most numerous of all survival foods and include dandelion, fireweed, dock, mountain sorrel, and nettle (boil young nettle leaves in water to remove the stinging chemicals). In addition, the young tender leaves of nearly all nonpoisonous plants are edible. Some plants with edible leaves have an edible pith in the center of the stem. Examples include buri, fishtail,

sago, coconut, rattan, and sugar cane. Edible flowers include abal, wild rose, colocynth, papaya, banana, horseradish, wild caper, and luffa sponge. Pollen looks like yellow dust and is high in nutritional value.

Fruits are among the most accessible and valuable plant foods. There are many kinds of edible fruits, both of the sweet and non-sweet (vegetable) type. Sweet fruits include crab apples, wild strawberry, wild cherry, blackberry, and cranberry. Vegetables include breadfruit, horseradish, rowan, and wild caper.

The grains of all cereals and other grasses are good sources of plant protein. They can be ground up and mixed with water to make porridge.

Pine needle tea

When crushed down and steeped in boiled water, pine needles provide a refreshing and nutritious tea. Select only the youngest and freshest needles.

Crush the needles down

Leave in hot boiled water for 10 minutes

Strain through a cloth to remove the needles

Plants that have edible seeds as well as grains include amaranth, Italian millet, rice, bamboo, nipa palm, tamarind, screw pine, water lily, and purslane.

Nuts are an excellent source of survival protein. Most can be eaten raw, though some, such as acorns, are better when cooked (boil acorns several times, replacing the water to remove the acorns' bitter taste). Plants with edible nuts include almond, water chestnut, beechnut, oak, pine, chestnut, cashew, hazelnut, and walnut.

Poisonous plants

You must have a knowledge of the most common types of poisonous plants so you can diligently avoid them. In particular, learn to identify hemlock and water hemlock, two of the deadliest and most widespread. Water hemlock has purplish stems; a hollow-chamb rootstalk; small, toothed, and 2–3 lobed leaflets; and clusters of small white flowers. It is always found near water and carries as unpleasant odor. Hemlock grows up to 6 feet (2m) high, and is multibranched with hollow, purple-

U.S. AIR FORCE TIPS: CAN YOU EAT THIS PLANT?

Use these simple U.S. Air Force guidelines, drawn up for downed pilots, when selecting plants for possible consumption in the wild. They will serve you well in a survival situation.

- Avoid plants with umbrella-shaped flowers, though carrots, celery, and parsley (all edible) are members of this family.
- Avoid all legumes (beans and peas); they absorb minerals from the soil and cause digestive problems.
- If in doubt, avoid all bulbs.
- Avoid all white and yellow berries—they are poisonous; half of all red berries are poisonous; blue or black berries are generally safe to eat.
- Aggregated fruits and berries are edible.
- Single fruits on a stem are considered safe to eat.
- A milky sap indicates a poisonous plant.
- Plants that are irritants to the skin should not be eaten.
- Plants that grow in water or moist soil are often very tasty.

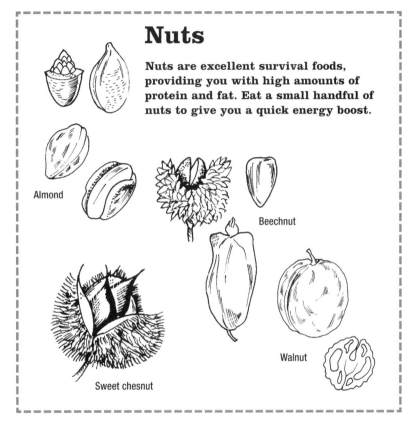

Nuts

Nuts are excellent survival foods, providing you with high amounts of protein and fat. Eat a small handful of nuts to give you a quick energy boost.

Almond

Beechnut

Sweet chesnut

Walnut

spotted stems and coarsely toothed leaves. It features dense clusters of tiny white flowers and white roots, and is found growing in grassy waste places throughout the world.

Other highly poisonous plants include the following:

– Poison ivy
– Baneberry
– Poison sumac
– Death camas
– Thorn-apple or jimson weed
– Foxglove
– Monk's-hood
– Deadly nightshade
– Buttercups
– Lupins
– Vetches or locoweeds
– Larkspur
– Henbane
– Nightshade berries

Poisonous plants

Poisonous plants sometimes give warning signs, such as aggressively colored berries or hairy, unappetizing looking stems. This is not always the case, however, so be careful when identifying survival plant foods.

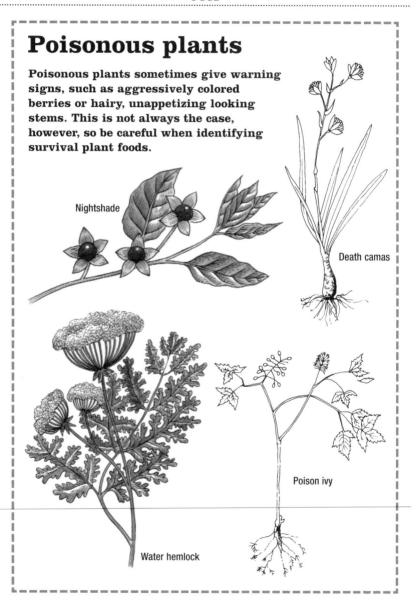

Nightshade

Death camas

Water hemlock

Poison ivy

Spend some time with a respected field guide getting to know these plants, and always remember never to consume any plant that you can't positively identify or that you haven't proved safe.

Edible fungi

Eating fungi requires great care. Certain varieties are lethally poisonous. The following fungi are some varities that can be eaten with confidence:

Giant Puffball; Slippery Jack; Chanterelle; Field Mushroom; Horse Mushroom; Horn of Plenty. (Note: Do not eat any species of ground mushroom that stain yellow when they are cut. This is an indication of poisonous content.)

Tree fungi—Beefsteak Fungus; Polyporus Sulphureus; Dryad's Saddle; Oyster Fungus; Honey Fungus.

Edible fungi

Fungi have to be identified on a case-by-case basis because there are no general rules to identification. These are all relatively widespread edible fungus.

Brain fungus

Beefsteak fungus

Giant puffball

SAS TIPS: GUIDELINES FOR SELECTING EDIBLE FUNGI

You must be extremely careful selecting fungi to eat. Use the following SAS tips for when you are collecting fungi.

- Avoid any fungi with white gills, a cuplike appendage at the base of the stem (volva) and stem rings.
- Avoid any fungi that are decomposing or wormy.
- Unless positively identified, avoid altogether.

Poisonous fungi

The following poisonous fungus MUST NOT be eaten:

Yellow Staining Mushroom; Destroying Angel; Death Cap; Fly Agaric; Panther Cap; Leaden Entoloma.

Seaweed

Edible seaweed can be found in shallow waters anchored to the bottom of rocks, or can be found floating on the open seas. Sea

Poisonous fungi

Avoid the following fungi diligently, and clean your hands and skin carefully if you come into contact with them.

Death cap

Destroying angel

Panther cap

lettuce is a light green, kelp is olive-green, sugarwrack has long, flat yellow-brown fronds, Irish moss has purplish to olive-green fronds, dulse is purplish red, and lavers have red, purplish, or brown fronds.

FOOD FROM ANIMALS

Remember one thing about acquiring food from animals: never expend more energy getting the food than you receive from it once you have caught and cooked it. Learn about the types of animals that inhabit the area you are in, including their tracks, habits, and where they sleep.

Unless you have a gun, you will get most of your game via snares and traps, and most of what you will catch in this way will be small animals and birds. If you do have a gun, observe the following rules when hunting prey: keep quiet; move slowly, stop frequently, and listen; be observant; hunt upwind or crosswind

Hunting rifles

Rifles are good for the long-range killing of medium–large sized animals, while shotguns have much shorter ranges but are better used against fast-moving targets.

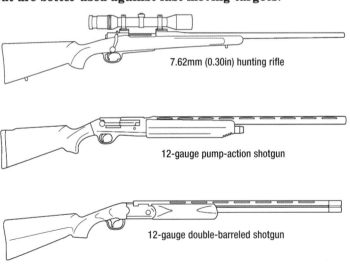

7.62mm (0.30in) hunting rifle

12-gauge pump-action shotgun

12-gauge double-barreled shotgun

Animal tracks

The patterning of animal tracks will help you identify what the animal is, how fast it is walking or running, and its direction of travel. The distance between prints will increase with the speed of movement.

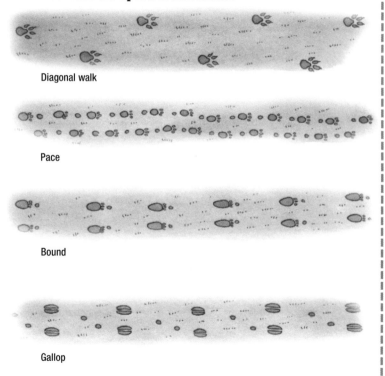

Diagonal walk

Pace

Bound

Gallop

whenever possible; blend in with the terrain features if you can. Be prepared. Game often startles the hunter and catches him off guard, resulting in a badly aimed shot.

Improvised hunting weapons
Bow and arrows: Select the best wood for your survival bow. Tension in unseasoned wood is short-lived— make several bows and change when

Animal footprints

Unless the animal has stepped in fresh mud, it is unusual to find tracks as perfect as those below. Often you might have to use several tracks to build up a composite picture.

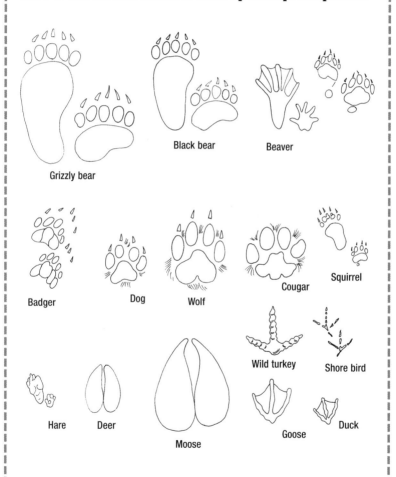

Grizzly bear

Black bear

Beaver

Badger

Dog

Wolf

Cougar

Squirrel

Hare

Deer

Moose

Wild turkey

Shore bird

Goose

Duck

Bow and arrows

A basic survival bow will have a short effective range, but good arrows will increase its lethality.

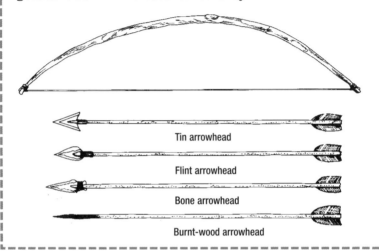

Tin arrowhead

Flint arrowhead

Bone arrowhead

Burnt-wood arrowhead

the one you are using loses its spring. Yew is best, but you may have to use other wood depending on the area you are in. The stave should be about 4 feet (120cm) long. Shape it so it is 2 inches (5cm) wide at the center and tapers to a half-inch (1.25cm) at the ends. Notch the ends in by a half-inch (1.25cm) to take the string. Rub the bow all over with oil or animal fat.

For the string, rawhide is best, though any string will do. When strung, the string should be under only slight tension: you provide the rest when you pull to shoot. Secure the string to the bow using a round turn and two half hitches.

Arrows should be made from straight wood 2 feet (60cm) long and a quarter-inch (6mm) wide. They should be as smooth and straight as possible. Notch one end a quarter-inch (6mm) deep to fit the bow string. Arrow flights can be made from feathers, paper, light cloth, or leaves trimmed to shape. If you split a feather down the center of the quill, leave three-quarters of an inch (20mm) of quill at each end of feather to tie to the arrow. It is best to tie three flights equally spaced around

Making a bow

Select a piece of wood that is flexible enough to draw comfortably within your strength, but which exerts tension throughout the length of the pull.

Select a stave that has no flaws or splits

Tie the bowstring with several looping knots

Note the swelling palm-grip section

the shaft. Arrowheads can be made of tin, flint, bone, or the wood burned black. Do not forget to put a notch in the end of each arrow to fit over your bowstring.

To shoot a bow, place an arrow in the bowstring and raise the center of the bow to the level of your eyes. Hold the bow in the center of the stave with your left hand (if you are right-handed) and rest the arrow on top of your hand. Keep this arm locked as you pull

Shot placement on a deer

Accurate shot placement is critical to bring down a deer effectively. Generally, always aim for the shoulder area.

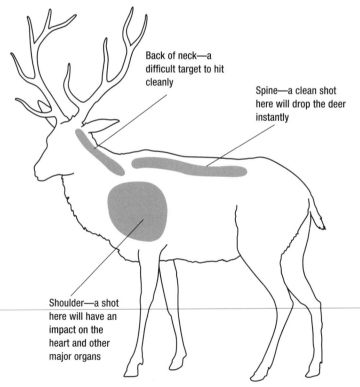

Back of neck—a difficult target to hit cleanly

Spine—a clean shot here will drop the deer instantly

Shoulder—a shot here will have an impact on the heart and other major organs

the bowstring back with your other hand, and keep the arrow at eye level while you are doing this. Line up the target with the arrow and release the string smoothly—do not snatch at the string as you release it. If you are hunting, it helps to have several arrows with you. Try to carry them in some sort of quiver and try to keep them dry.

Spears: These can be used to catch fish and game. They can be quite

Spears

By changing the spearhead, the spear can be adapted to hunting different types of hunting.

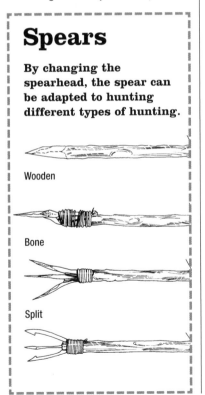

Wooden

Bone

Split

CANADIAN SPECIAL FORCES TIPS: WHAT TO LOOK FOR WHEN HUNTING

Canada's elite troops are adept at locating animals for food in the frozen wastes of their country by being alert and aware of animal habits.

- Animals will be unsure when they see you. Remain still, make slow movements, and if you have a gun make the first shot count.
- Follow trails beaten down by heavy usage.
- Tracks and droppings can provide information on the type, size, age, and sex of animals.
- Feeding grounds and water holes are good sites for hunting in the early morning or evening. Trails leading to them can be set with snares or traps.
- Dens, holes, and food stores are good sites for setting snares.

Spiked harpoon

The spiked harpoon is an excellent weapon for fishing. Its multiple heads grip slippery prey firmly.

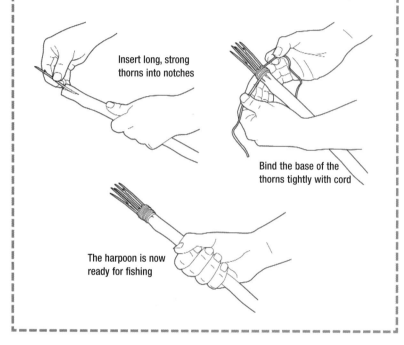

Insert long, strong thorns into notches

Bind the base of the thorns tightly with cord

The harpoon is now ready for fishing

simple—e.g. a stick with a sharpened point, though this can break or dull easily. You can also improvise spearheads from antler or animal bones, flint, or tin.

For catching fish, split the end of the spear into three sharpened pieces and put in spacer blocks to keep them spread apart, or fit the spearhead with three long, sharp thorns or pieces of bones. This type of spear will provide better grip on a slippery fish than a spear with a single head.

Catapult: Select a strong Y-shaped branch and a piece of elastic material (a piece of inner-tube from a tire is ideal). Make a pouch for the center of the elastic and thread or

Spear thrower

The spear thrower is designed to give additional force and, therefore, range and penetration behind a spear throw. Much practice is required to combine this extra force with good accuracy over distance.

The spear sits in the channel carved into the wood

All the body weight should be put behind the throw

Catapult

A powerful catapult will comfortably kill small creatures such as birds, squirrels, and rabbits. Its advantage is that it does not require lengthy practice to achieve decent accuracy.

sew it into position. Tie the ends of each side of the branch. Use stones or small rocks as missiles. With practice, you can become very accurate and deadly against any type of target.

Slingshot: A slingshot can be nothing more than a long piece of rope or leather thong with a pouch in the middle to hold the ammunition (small, smooth stones are ideal). To use a slingshot, swing the sling above your head and release one end of the thong to send the ammunition in the direction of the target. When you are using a catapult or slingshot to bring down birds, use several stones at once.

Bola: Wrap stones in material and knot each one with pieces of cord 3 feet (90cm) long. Tie all the pieces together. Hold at the joined end and then twirl around the head, building up speed until it is released at the target. It can be used against birds in flight or on animal's legs, giving you a chance to close in for the kill when the animal is disabled.

When using weapons to kill prey, try to stalk the creature as close as possible, then use the weapon with focused violence. Be careful what types of prey you tackle. Avoid tackling large, dangerous creatures such as bears and large cattle unless you have an appropriate gun or very

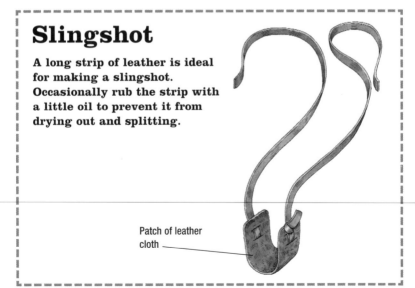

Slingshot

A long strip of leather is ideal for making a slingshot. Occasionally rub the strip with a little oil to prevent it from drying out and splitting.

Patch of leather cloth

Bola

A bola is useful for bringing down animals on the run because the strings and weights tangle the legs.

U.S. Army Rangers are taught how to overcome their natural fear of snakes and turn the animal into a tasty and nutritious meal.

- Trap the animal by pinning it to the ground with a forked twig just behind the head. Kill by clubbing.
- Grip dead snake firmly behind the head.
- Cut off the head with a knife.
- Slit open belly and remove innards.
- Skin snake (use skin for improvising belts and straps).

powerful bow and know how to use it. Be careful of attempting to kill the young of such species—an aggressive mother could be close by. Even smaller animals require careful handling. Squirrels, weasels, stoats, mink, martens, and polecats are all trappable, but a wounded individual will fight violently if you attempt to pick it up, and can deliver significant injuries. A smack to the head with a heavy stick should be enough to ensure the animal is safe to handle.

TRAPPING ANIMALS

Trapping is particularly suited to catching mammals such as rabbits, squirrels, foxes, and deer. The type of trap, and more importantly, the size, should be pitched at the animal you want to catch.

Snares

A snare is a wire or string loop placed in such a way that an animal is forced to put its head through it. The snare will then tighten, thus holding the animal or killing it (though sometimes not immediately). If you

Types of snare

Wire or cord can be used to make snares, but generally wire is preferred, being more easily concealed and locking more effectively.

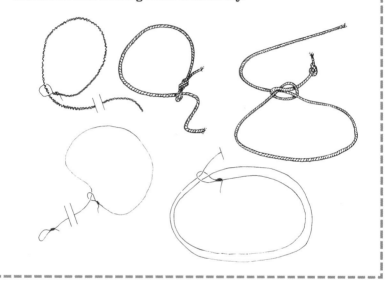

are setting snares, you should check them regularly for trapped animals and to ensure that they are working (and also to prevent kills being stolen by other predators). Some commercial snares are self-locking. Homemade snares are just as effective, but the material you make the snare out of must be strong enough to hold its intended prey.

Your aims when positioning snares are: keep the loop open and unrestricted so it can tighten on the animal, and keep it a proper distance off the ground. Do not walk on animal trails when setting the snare—your scent will discourage the animal from moving into the trap.

Remember, wire snares are easy to position because of their rigidity.

Snares should be sited as follows:
- On heavily used trails or in an area where animals are feeding on vegetation or on a carcass.
- Near a den or well used stores of food.

Simple snare

Note how the snare wire is raised off the ground to the height of the animal's head.

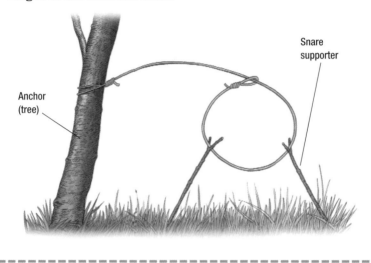

Anchor (tree)

Snare supporter

• Position foliage in such a way that it will force animals to pass through your snares.

Deadfall traps
The principle of these traps is simple. When the bait is taken, a weight falls on the prey and kills it. There are many types of deadfall triggers, but they are all activated by a tripline release action or by a baited release action. With the tripline release, the animal trips a line, stick, or pole, activating the deadfall. With the baited release, the animal is attracted to the deadfall by the bait, then pulls on the bait, making the deadfall drop. See the illustrations in this chapter for examples of deadfall traps and their triggers. When making deadfall traps, never position yourself beneath the weight or you could be the trap's first victim.

Spear traps
These traps can be very effective. They consist of a springy shaft that is held in place by a tripline, with a spear being firmly lashed to the springy shaft, which hits the animal when released.

Deadfall traps (1)

Deadfall traps can use single killing weights (bottom) or multiple weights (top) to improve the chances of a hit.

Trigger mechanism

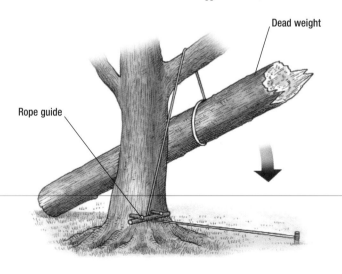

Dead weight

Rope guide

Deadfall traps (2)

The trigger is the most critical part of a deadfall trap. It must be sensitive to touch, but resistant to simple collapse and to being blown down by the wind.

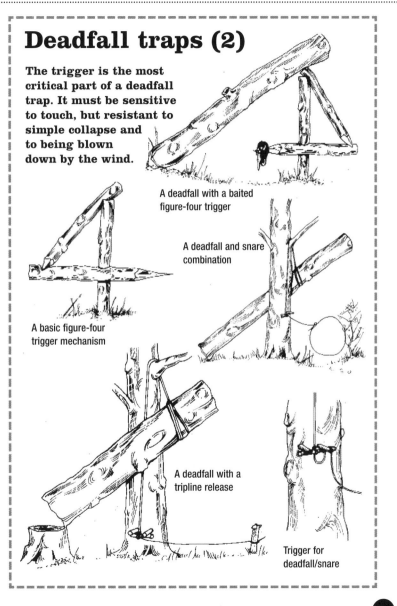

A deadfall with a baited figure-four trigger

A deadfall and snare combination

A basic figure-four trigger mechanism

A deadfall with a tripline release

Trigger for deadfall/snare

MAKING A FIGURE-FOUR TRIGGER

The figure-four trigger is one of the easiest triggers to make and use in deadfall traps.

For the upright stick:
- cut the top at an angle and square off the tip to enable it to fit into a notch in the release stick.
- cut a square notch near the bottom to fit a corresponding square notch in the bait stick. Flatten the sides of the stick at this notch to guarantee a good fit with the bait stick.

For the release stick:
- cut the top so the deadfall will rest on it securely until triggered.
- cut a notch near the top in which to fit the upright stick.
- cut the bottom end at an angle to fit into the bait stick.

For the bait stick
- cut a notch near one end, in which to place the end of the release stick.
- shape the other end to hold the bait.
- cut a square notch at the spot where it crosses the upright stick; the notches in the upright stick and the bait stick should fit firmly together.
- rest the trigger on a stone or a piece of wood to stop it from sinking into the ground.

Bird traps

There are several effective ways of catching birds. One way is to put a stone in a piece of bait and throw it into the air. A bird will attempt to swallow it, but the stone will catch in

WARNING: SPEAR TRAPS CAN KILL. ALWAYS APPROACH THEM FROM BEHIND.

Spear traps

Spear traps should be set so that when released they sweep across the kill zone consistently at a chosen height. Make sure the size of the spikes relates to the size of the prey you are attempting to kill.

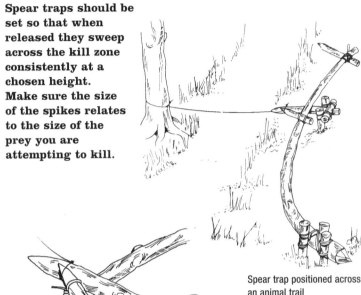

Spear trap positioned across an animal trail

Make sure the spear is firmly tied onto the springy shaft

its mouth, causing it to fall to earth, where you can club it. The following traps will also serve you well:

- Suspended snares—hang a line of snares across a stream above water level.

- Baited hooks—fish hooks that have been hidden in fruit or other food are a good method of catching birds. When the birds swallow the bait, the hooks catch in their throats.

SAS TIPS: EATING INSECTS

All SAS soldiers are taught how to catch and prepare insects to eat. Adhere to their guidelines when searching for insects.

- Be careful when searching for insects: their hiding places may also conceal scorpions, spiders, and snakes.
- Do not eat insects that have fed on dung: they carry infection.
- Do not eat brightly colored insects: they are typically poisonous.
- Do not collect grubs found on the underside of leaves: they secrete poisonous fluids.
- Cook ants for at least six minutes to destroy the poisons that are found in some types. Boil all insects caught in water in case the water is polluted.
- When eating crickets or locusts, remove the head, legs, and wings before eating.

Finding insect food

Insect food is usually accessible, especially in tropical climates. Termites provide good nutrition, though penetrating their rock-hard nests takes some work. Illustrated is one technique, but another involves simply smashing your way in with a rock.

Push a long stick into the termite nest

74

Draw out the stick, and scrape off any insects clinging to it

• Noose sticks—tie a number of nooses a half-inch to 1 inch (1.25 to 2.5cm) in diameter close together along a branch or stick. Position in a favorite roosting or nesting spot. Birds become entangled when they alight.

Preparing a mammal

After you have killed a mammal, slit its throat to bleed it. Try to save the blood, which is full of vitamins and minerals. Place the carcass belly up. Cut around the anus, and if the animal is a male cut the skin parallel to, but not touching, the penis. (For rabbits, first squeeze the abdomen in a downward direction with your thumbs to expel any urine from the bladder.) Insert the first two fingers between the skin and the membrane enclosing the entrails. Place the knife blade between the two fingers and extend the cut to the chin. Cut the diaphragm at the ribcage; cut the pelvic bone and remove the anus; and split open the breast and remove as much of the windpipe as possible. Turn the animal on its side and roll out the entrails (or shake them out in the case of a rabbit).

Once an animal is gutted, it can usually be skinned. Cut off the lower legs at the joints, slit down the insides of the legs, and then work the skin off the carcass, moving from the rear of the animal to the head.

Apart from the lean meat on the animal, you can use the following

Gutting a deer

Gutting and preparing a deer is hard work, but the volumes of meat provided are rewarding. Be careful with the knife because it is easy to slip off bone or sinew. Make sure the blade is razor sharp.

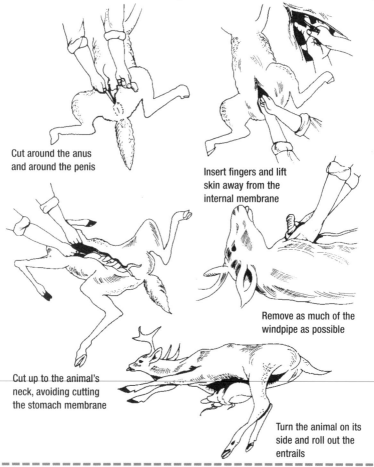

Cut around the anus and around the penis

Insert fingers and lift skin away from the internal membrane

Remove as much of the windpipe as possible

Cut up to the animal's neck, avoiding cutting the stomach membrane

Turn the animal on its side and roll out the entrails

Skinning a rabbit

With practice, skinning a rabbit can be done quickly and efficiently. Keep the fur you remove—it can be used to make pieces of clothing.

Draw the skin downward over the lower body

Having gutted the rabbit, make incisions around the rear legs

Keep working the skin apart toward the head; cut off the front feet

Pull the skin in one piece over the top of the rabbit's head

parts of the animal for food or for other applications:

- Blood—a good base for soups.

- Entrails, heart, liver, and kidney— all edible if not discolored.
- Fat—good for making soups.
- Skin—makes leather for clothing.

Draining the blood

Animal blood is full of nutrients, and should not be wasted when preparing an animal. Blood can be added to soups and stocks as a nutritious thickening agent.

- Tendons and ligaments—can be used for lashings.
- Bone marrow—a rich food source.
- Bones—can be used for making tools and weapons.

Fishing

Fishing can be invaluable for the survivor. There are fish in the seas, rivers, and lakes in all parts of the world, and they can be caught relatively easily. The hooks and lead weights in your survival kit are truly worth their weight in gold, and the illustrations here also show methods of improvising hooks and line. Employ the fishing methods listed below to catch fish using your line, weights, and hooks. You should improvise a gaff hook (see illustration) to land large fish.

Still fishing

Weight your line with a float, lead weight, or a rock. Attach a baited hook or hooks and let it settle on the bottom of the river or float. Take up the slack and wait for a strike, but tug on the line occasionally.

Making fishing hooks

A thorn or piece of metal can be converted into an effective fishing hook.

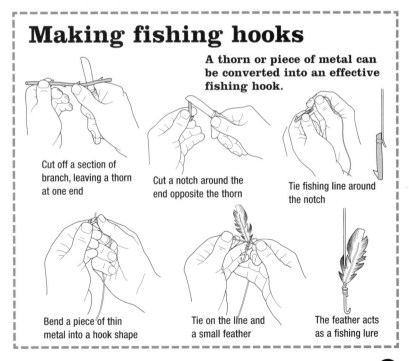

Cut off a section of branch, leaving a thorn at one end

Cut a notch around the end opposite the thorn

Tie fishing line around the notch

Bend a piece of thin metal into a hook shape

Tie on the line and a small feather

The feather acts as a fishing lure

Finding fish

Fish can be attracted to shaded patches of a river or, in colder climates, sunny areas. They often swim downstream of a breakwater object such as a gravel bank or rock, taking advantage of the slower current there.

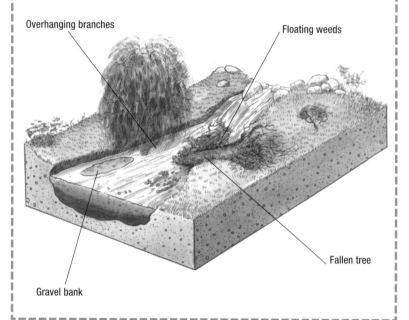

Overhanging branches

Floating weeds

Fallen tree

Gravel bank

Dry-fly fishing

This method is used when fish feed off the surface of the water. Improvise a line with a stick, a piece of string or line. Cast the fly upstream and let it float down past you. Experiment with the size and colors of your flies. Remember that this method of fishing cannot be used in very cold weather when there are no airborne insects around (the fish will not bite).

Set lining

This involves casting a long line with several baited hooks into the water and leaving it overnight. Put out two

Keeping out of sight

The refraction of light through water means a fish can see what's on the riverbank at a very sharp angle. Stay low to ensure that you don't scare away the fish.

Fish's line of sight

Basket trap

By channeling the flow of the water into the mouth of the basket trap, you can catch large quantities of fish very quickly. For that reason, check the basket trap at least every hour to see what you have caught.

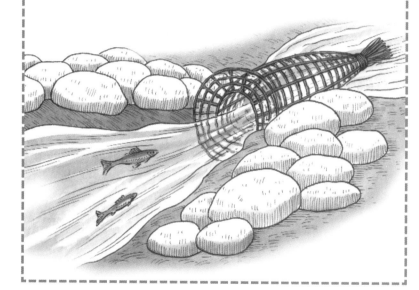

lines, one on the bottom and one off the bottom.

Gill netting

Here you construct a net to catch fish by their gills as they try to swim through it. It is very effective for streams; tie stones along the bottom edge of the net to keep it on the bottom. Alternatively, make a

trap with stones or rocks and herd fish into it.

Filleting fish

To fillet a fish for cooking, first slit the fish from the anus to just behind the gills and remove the internal organs by pulling them out with your fingers. Wash and clean the flesh, then trim off the fins and tail. Cut

Running line and float line

A running line enables you to keep fishing without actually being present. Set multiple fishing lines at different depths to maximize your chances of a catch.

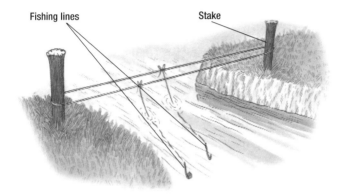

Fishing lines

Stake

In the first configuration, the bait is attached to a float with a short length of line. In the lower example, a stone is used to lower the bait to catch fish nearer the seabed.

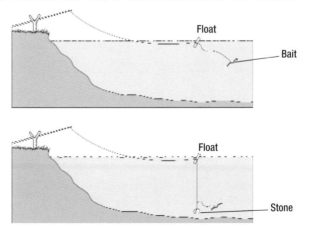

Float

Bait

Float

Stone

Filleting fish

Filleting fish requires a very sharp knife. If you don't have such a tool, it is best to cook fish whole rather than attempt the filleting process.

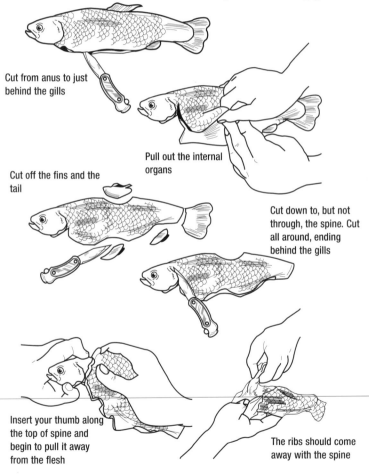

Cut from anus to just behind the gills

Pull out the internal organs

Cut off the fins and the tail

Cut down to, but not through, the spine. Cut all around, ending behind the gills

Insert your thumb along the top of spine and begin to pull it away from the flesh

The ribs should come away with the spine

FISHING TIPS

The soldiers of all elite units are taught how to catch fish in the wild. Try to use these guidelines when you are in a survival situation.

- Use natural bait whenever possible.
- Do not use too big a hook for the type of fish you are trying to catch; better too small than too big.
- Remember how you were fishing when you get a strike; continue with this method.
- If you are not catching fish, change your methods and/or your lures.
- Save the eyes and entrails for the next day's fishing.
- Try spear fishing—it can be very effective.
- Fish become more active feeders when there is a change in the weather.
- Do not eat shellfish that are not covered by water at high tide.

down to, but not through, the spine. Cut around the spine, finishing behind the gills on both sides. Insert your thumb along the top of the spine and begin to pull it away from the flesh. The ribs should come out cleanly with the spine. If the flesh does not come away cleanly and you find you are wasting too much good meat by attempting to fillet the fish, simply gut the fish, wash it thoroughly, and cook whole.

STORING AND PREPARING FOOD

If you kill more animals than you can eat, you have to store the food properly for later consumption. In winter, you can freeze the meat. After dividing the meat into sections, you should build a cache to store it in. Construct a platform off the ground and cover the meat placed on it with boughs to keep birds away. Do not build your cache in your camp. In the summer it may attract bears, and the last thing you want is a hungry bear sniffing around your camp looking for food.

Unless you are going to eat the meat immediately, you will want to preserve it. Cooling preserves meat: try to keep your catch as cool as possible. Cut the meat into sections

Carrying a carcass

For carrying a heavy carcass over long distances, try using the method pictured here. Tie the torso as close to the pole as possible to reduce swinging effects.

Smoking

A smoking frame such as this one lets the smoke move evenly around the food. Use green leaves on the fire to generate a thick smoke.

Storing

Hide a large carcass in a tree for short-term storage.

and hang them in a cool place out of the sun. The air will start to dry the outside of the meat and will cool it at the same time.

Start a number of smoky fires to smoke the meat. Do not let the fires heat the meat: just smoke it (do not use conifer wood—it ruins the flavor). Smoked meat, if kept cool and dry, can be stored in this condition for a long time.

Dry smoking preserves the meat even longer. Cut the meat up into long, thin strips and hang them on a drying rack. Dry the meat out in sunlight or with a fire. At the same time, have a smoky hardwood fire

Drying frame

Make a simple drying frame for air-drying meats and vegetables, but watch it closely in case animals attempt to steal your food.

SAS TIPS: RULES FOR AVOIDING DISEASED ANIMALS

Avoid eating animals suffering from disease. Follow these rules, which are used by the British SAS, for identifying ill animals.

- Check lymph glands (in the cheek). If they are large and discolored, the animal is ill.
- Animals that are distorted or discolored around the head are diseased; their meat should be boiled thoroughly.
- Cover any cut or sore in your skin when preparing diseased animals.

Cooking on hot rocks

Heated rocks can make a grill surface for cooking strips of meat, fish, and vegetables.

Make an even pile of large, smooth rocks

Brush the embers from the rocks using branche

going. When the meat seems dry, move it nearer the fire for a few minutes to raise the temperature. When the strips are hot to the touch, move them back from the fire and continue to dry them until they become very brittle.

In this state, they will last a long time. You can chew on them or cook them in water to rehydrate them.

COOKING

The main types of cooking are boiling, frying, parching, baking, steaming, and roasting, and you can employ them all in the wild.

Boiling

Boil in a metal container, in a rock with a hole in it (not rocks with a high moisture content, though, which

Build a fire on top of the rocks and then let it burn down

Lay the food directly onto the rocks to cook

EXPLOSIVE ROCKS

Do not place wet or porous rocks and stones near fires—they can explode when heated. Do not use slates and soft rocks, or any that crack, sound hollow, or flake. Test all rocks by banging them together. Any moisture in the rock will expand faster than the rock itself when heated and may explode, with potentially lethal effects.

can explode and inflict serious injuries), or in a hollowed-out piece of wood (hang the wood over the fire and add hot rocks to the water and food, replacing them as they cool with hot ones until the food cooks). Food can also be boiled in coconut shells, seashells, turtle shells, and half sections of bamboo. You can make a boiling pot by scooping a hole in hard ground, lining it with leaves or other waterproof material, filling it with water, and then dropping red-hot coals from the fire into it.

Frying
Skillets can be formed from desert rocks. Find a flat and narrow rock, then prop it up with other rocks and build a fire underneath it. Make sure you wipe off all the grit and dirt before you heat it. The rock will heat up, enabling you to fry meat or eggs (raid birds' nests to get them) on it.

Parching
This works well with nuts and grains. Place in a container or on a rock and heat slowly until they are scorched.

Baking in mud

Baking food in mud is a gentle way of cooking fish and other meats. The outer layers of mud and leaves protect the food from burning.

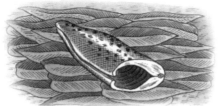

Wrap the fish in a thick layer of green leaves

Tie the leaves in places with cordage

Cover the parcel with a thick layer of mud or soil

Make a large fire on and around the parcel; by the time the fire burns down, the food inside the parcel should be cooked

Baking

Improvise an oven by using a pit under a fire, a closed container, or a wrapping of leaves or clay. Another method of baking is to line a pit with moisture-free stones and build a fire in the pit. As the fire burns down, scrape the coals back and put the covered container in, then cover it with a layer of coals and a thin layer of dirt. This will enable the food to bake.

Mud baking is a good way to cook small animals. First clean the carcass by removing the head, feet, and tail, but leave on the skin or feathers. Cover the carcass with mud or clay at least 1 inch (2.5cm) thick, then place in a fire and cover with coals. Depending on its size, the animal may take up to 1 hour to cook. When the clay is bricklike and hard, remove it from the fire. Break open the covering. The feathers or skin will break away at the same time, leaving a ready meal.

Yukon stove

The Yukon stove is a good structure to build if you intend to stay in one place for some time. Cook over the open chimney or by inserting wrapped foods into the "oven" at the bottom.

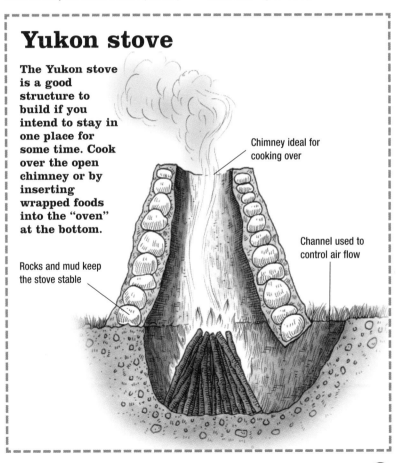

Chimney ideal for cooking over

Channel used to control air flow

Rocks and mud keep the stove stable

Hobo stove

A simple oil drum can be converted into a stove. Cut a fuel port and ventilation holes in the bottom. The top of the drum can be used for frying.

Roasting

Roasting is done with a skewer or spit over an open fire. It is a good method for cooking whole fowls or small animals.

Grilling

Dig a hole larger and wider than the animal to be cooked, approximately 1 to 3 feet (30 to 60cm) deep. Build a fire at the bottom of it and wait until it is hot. Then spread green poles over the top of the hole and place the meat on top of them. You can put small stones in the fire to radiate the heat.

Earth oven

This method of cooking is used in the South Seas. Dig a hole

SAS SURVIVAL TIPS: SURVIVAL COOKING

SAS soldiers are expert at turning even the most unlikely looking and seemingly inedible creature into a tasty and nutritious meal.

- Meat: cut into small cubes and boil. Treat pork in warm climates with caution because wild pigs are infested with worms and liver fluke, and venison is also prone to worms.
- Fish: usually germ-free if caught in fresh water; best stewed or wrapped in leaves and baked.
- Birds: boil all carrion; young birds can be roasted.
- Reptiles: gut and cook in their skins in hot embers; when skin splits, remove and boil; cut off snake heads before cooking because some have venom glands in their heads. Skin frogs (many have poisonous skins) and roast on a stick.
- Turtles and tortoises: boil until shell comes off; cut up meat and cook until tender.
- Shellfish: boil crabs, lobsters, shrimp, and crayfish to remove harmful organisms. All seafood spoils quickly, so cook as soon as possible.
- Insects and worms: can be boiled, or dried on hot rocks, then crushed and ground into a powder to add to soups and stews.

2 feet (60cm) wide and 2 feet (60cm) deep. Gather some wood and make a criss-cross pattern over the hole, laying one layer of sticks in one direction and one layer in another. Then lay a number of medium-sized stones on top of the sticks. Start a fire in the hole and let it burn until the stones turn white and fall into the hole. Arrange the stones in the hole and shovel out any pieces of burning wood, then cover the stones

Mud oven

The mud oven is an ideal roasting machine, though it does require a large fireproof pot. When building the oven, make sure you leave a gap in the trench under the pot for the fire.

Dig a narrow trench, and lay a fireproof pot along it. Jam a stick into the ground at the base of the pot.

with a lot of green leaves that have been moistened with water and throw the food to be cooked on top. Cover the food with another batch of leaves and then cover the hole with earth to ensure no steam escapes.

After about two hours, the food will be cooked. This is an excellent method of cooking but requires speed when you are arranging the stones to ensure that they do not cool.

Cover the body of the pot with a thick layer of soil. When you have finished, remove the stick (the hole acts as as a chimney).

Lid held on with a stick

Light a fire beneath the pot. This will heat the interior of the pot to ovenlike temperatures.

Fire is extremely important to survival. It is a great morale booster, keeps you warm, dries your clothes, boils water, and can be used for signaling and for cooking food. It is imperative that you know how to build, start, and maintain a fire.

MAKING FIRE

The materials for a fire fall into three categories: tinder, kindling, and fuel. Tinder is any type of material that has a low flash point and is easily ignited. It usually consists of thin, bone-dry fibers. Tinder includes shredded bark from some trees and bushes; crushed fibers from dead plants; fine, dry wood shavings, straw and grasses; resinous sawdust; very fine pitch wood shavings; bird or rodent nest linings; seed down; charred cloth; cotton balls or lint; steel wool; dry powdered sap from pine trees; paper; and foam rubber.

Get into the habit of always having tinder with you, and remember to carry it in a waterproof container.

Kindling has a higher combustible point and is added to the tinder. It is used to bring the burning

. . . .

Left: Survival firemaking is not just about creating flames from techniques such as the bow-drill method (top). It is also about creating the right type of fire for your purposes, and keeping that fire going under poor conditions.

4

Making fire in the wild means rediscovering some very ancient survival skills.

Making Fire

Fire plow

The fire plow creates smoldering embers through friction generated by the stick rubbing up and down the groove of the hearth. Make the strokes long and fast, and use strong pressure.

Hearth

Groove

Tinder

temperature of the fire up to the point where less combustible fuel can be added to the fire. Kindling includes dead, small, dry twigs, coniferous seed cones and needles, and wood that has been doused with flammable materials.

Fuel doesn't have to be dry to burn, but moist wood will produce a lot of smoke. The best fuel sources are dry, dead wood and the insides of fallen trees and large branches (which may be dry even if the outside is wet). Green wood can be split and mixed with dry wood to be used as fuel. If there are no trees, twist dry grass into bunches, use dead cactus, dry peat moss, or dried animal dung.

Siting a fire

In forested and grassy areas, clear a wide circular area around the site of your fire, to prevent the fire from spreading to nearby foliage. Keep a stockpile of kindling and fuel close at hand.

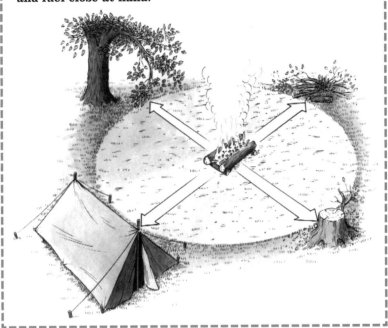

Fire sites

A site for your fire should be carefully selected. Remember that you want your fire to be a source of warmth, protection, and cooking facilities. If you have to build a fire in deep snow or marshy ground, build a temple fire. This consists of a platform of green logs with earth on top raised above the ground by four uprights at each corner, which have cross-pieces in their forks for the platform to rest on.

If you can, build a fire reflector (which is simply a kind of wall) out of logs or rocks. It will direct or reflect the heat where you want it and will reduce the amount of wind that may be blowing into the fire. You can also

SAS TIPS: RULES FOR FIRE SITES

It is important to have a good spot for your fire. The SAS has many years of experience of building survival fires in all types of terrain. Some advice:

- Choose a sheltered site.
- Do not light a fire at the base of a stump or tree.
- Clear away all debris on the ground from a circle at least 6 feet (2m) cross until you reveal bare earth.
- If the ground is wet or covered with snow, build the fire on a platform constructed from green logs covered with a layer of earth or stones.
- In strong winds, dig a trench and light a fire in it.
- In windy conditions, encircle your fire with rocks.

use reflectors to direct heat into your sleeping shelter.

Do not build a fire up against a rock. Instead, position it so you can sit between the rock and the fire. For even greater warmth, build a reflector beyond the fire that directs warmth back toward you (the rock will absorb warmth and keep your back warm).

Starting fires without matches

Survivors must know how to start a fire without matches in a long-term survival situation. There are a number of easy ways to make fire without commercial matches:

Flint and steel

Hold the flint and steel near the base of a ball of tinder (the ball should be at least the size of your fist). Strike the flint with the edge of the steel in a downward glance. The sparks must be directed onto the tinder and then further blown on or fanned to produce a subsequent flame.

Battery

If you have access to a battery, connect the end of one piece of insulated wire to the positive post and the end of another piece of insulated wire to the negative post. Touch the two remaining ends to the ends of a piece of noninsulated wire. The noninsulated wire will begin to glow and get hot, and can be used to ignite the kindling. Remember to move the battery away once you have the fire going.

Burning glass

Concentrate rays of the sun on tinder using a magnifying glass, a camera lens, the lens of a flashlight that magnifies, or even a convex piece of bottle glass. The heat will start ignition. Blow gently to encourage a flame.

Flashlamp reflector

Place tinder in the center of a flashlamp reflector, where the bulb is usually located. Push it up from the back of the hole until the hottest light is concentrated on the end and smoke results. If available, a cigarette can be used as tinder for this method.

Bow and Drill

This is an ancient method of making fire, and a useful one for the survivor to know. Make a spindle out of straight hardwood, the spindle to be around 12 to 18 inches (30 to 45cm)

Fire without matches

When people think of starting fires without matches, they often think of hand-drill or bow-drill methods. Yet there are many other techniques for making a flame.

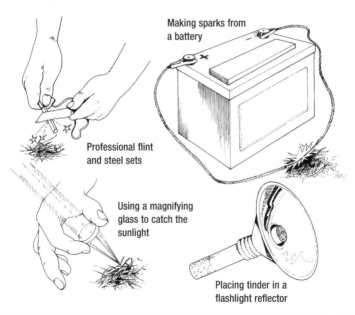

Making sparks from a battery

Professional flint and steel sets

Using a magnifying glass to catch the sunlight

Placing tinder in a flashlight reflector

long and three-quarters of an inch (1.9cm) in diameter. Round off one end and work the other into a blunt point. The round end goes into hole in a socket, which is made from hardwood and which can be held comfortably (put grease or soap in the hole to stop unwanted friction). Make the bow from a branch around 3 feet (90cm) long and 1 inch (2.5cm) in diameter. Tie a piece of suspension line or leather thong to both ends so it has the tension of a bow. The fireboard is made from softwood and is around 1 foot (30cm) long and three-quarters of an inch (1.9cm) thick and 3 to 6 inches (7.5 to 15cm) wide. Carve a small hollow in it, then make a V-shaped cut in from the edge of the board. It should extend into the

Hand drill

The hand-drill method of starting a fire requires considerable practice to master, and a lot of effort. Maintain a steady rhythm and don't take a break between sessions, otherwise the wood will cool down.

center of the hollow, where the spindle will make the hollow deeper. The object of the "V" is to create an angle that cuts off the edge of the spindle as it gets hot and produces charcoal dust.

While kneeling on one knee, place the other foot on the fireboard and place tinder just beneath the V-cut. Rest the board on two sticks to create the space (this allows air into the tinder). Twist the bow string once around the spindle and place the spindle upright into the hollow. Then press the socket down on the spindle and fireboard. Spin the spindle with long, even strokes of the bow until smoke is produced. By this stage a hot powder is created, which can be blown into a glowing ember. Then remove the bow and spindle and place tinder next to the glowing ember. Roll tinder around the burning ember and blow to draw out a flame. Then place the burning tinder in a waiting fire containing more tinder and small kindling.

TYPES OF FIRE

There are different types of fires, all used for specific purposes. You

Fire pit

Fire pits can prevent flames from catching on nearby foliage. The pit also provides an opening across which food can be grilled.

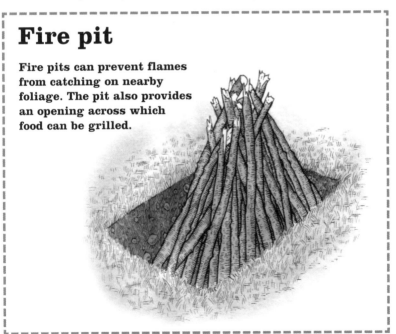

Tipi fire

This jumbled-up looking fire will burn fast and strong on account of its tall structure and the plentiful ventilation provided by its loose construction.

should learn how to site and build them all.

Safety night fire

This fire enables you to stay close to the fire while sleeping without the danger of burning logs rolling on you. Place two large, green logs against the fire, ensuring that as the fire burns it will be kept away from you and your shelter. Make sure the fire has as few air spaces as possible to ensure it burns throughout the night.

Long fire

This fire begins as a trench, which is dug to take advantage of the wind. However, it can also be constructed above ground by using two parallel green logs to hold the coals together. Make sure the logs are at least 6 inches (15cm) wide (though the thicker, the better) and positioned so that cooking utensils can be rested on them. Two 1 inch (2.5cm) diameter sticks can be placed under them to let the fire receive more air.

"T" fire

This fire is good for cooking. The fire is maintained in the top part of the "T," which provides coals for cooking in the bottom part of the "T."

Tipi

This is an excellent type of fire for

Windbreak

In windy conditions, build a windbreak around the fire. Here snowblocks have been used in a semi-circular pattern, but rocks and logs are more typical materials.

both cooking and heat, but you need to have ample supplies of fuel at the ready to maintain it. Place some tinder in the middle of the fire site and push a stick into the ground, slanting over the tinder. Lean a circle of kindling sticks against the slanting stick, with an opening toward the wind to let in a draft. Light the fire with your back to the wind and feed the fire from the downwind side.

Star fire

This is used to conserve fuel supplies or if you want only a small fire. The fire is in the center of the "wheel"; push the logs in according to requirements. Drawn them apart if you want to cook over embers. Hardwood is best for this type of fire.

Keyhole fire

Dig a hole in the ground in the shape of a key, taking advantage of the

U.S. SPECIAL FORCES TIPS: FIRECRAFT TIPS

Use these very simple rules, employed by American elite soldiers, for making and siting fires in the wilderness.

- Reserve your matches for starting properly prepared fires, not for lighting cigarettes or improperly prepared fires.
- Always try to carry dry tinder in a waterproof container.
- In the Arctic, a platform will be needed to prevent fire from melting down through deep snow and putting itself out.
- You will also need a platform if you start a fire in an area of peat or humus to stop it spreading. A smoldering peat fire can continue burning for years.
- In woods, clear away ground debris to prevent fire from spreading.

wind. This fire does the same job as the long fire.

Pyramid fire
This is similar to the log-cabin fire (below), except that it uses layers of fuel instead of a hollow framework. This fire burns for a long time, which means that it can be used as an overnight fire.

Log cabin
The stacked structure of this fire produces great heat and light

Platform

In snowy conditions, make your fire on a platform of rocks or logs.

because of the amount of oxygen that enters it. As such, it can be used for cooking and signaling.

CARRYING FIRE

Carrying fire is an effective way of preserving your fire-starting materials and of saving you the bother of starting a fire when you decide to make camp for the night. As with everything else concerning survival, you should practice making fire bundles and tubes before you actually need them, and remember to have more than one ready to use.

The illustration on pages 108–109 shows two of the most effective ways of carrying fire, though you may only need to use fire tubes if you do not have a tin can.

Fire bundles

Place a number of hot coals, surrounded by dry tinder and then damp grass and leaves, in a medium-sized can with ventilation holes.

Carrying fire

Carrying fire from place to place saves you the hassle of starting new flames every time you make camp.

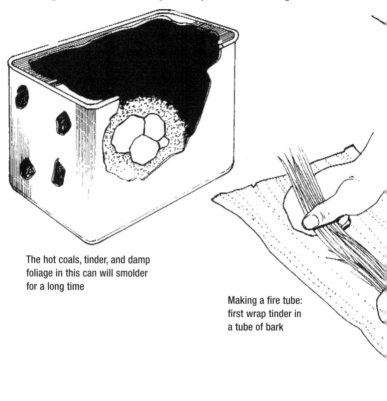

The hot coals, tinder, and damp foliage in this can will smolder for a long time

Making a fire tube: first wrap tinder in a tube of bark

Fire tube

Take a long sheet of bark and lay tinder down the middle. Roll the tube and secure it with ties all down its length. Drop embers into the end of the tube to start it smoldering. Keep the tube pointing into the breeze. If it catches fire, spit on it or stamp on it to regain control.

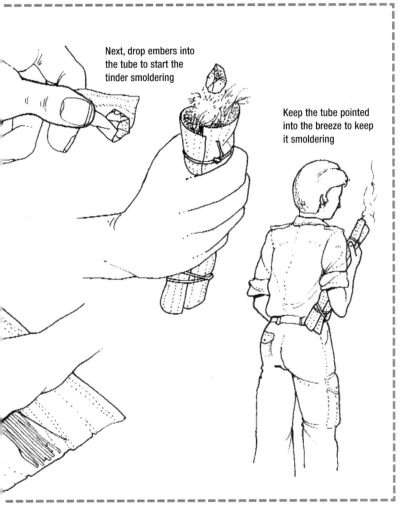

Next, drop embers into the tube to start the tinder smoldering

Keep the tube pointed into the breeze to keep it smoldering

There other ways of carrying fire, including transporting a burning log and swinging it to keep it alight (though if you are going to do this, make sure you are physically strong enough). Another method for transporting fire is to wrap a piece of coal in a fireproof leaf.

In a survival situation, you must find shelter or build your own to protect you from the wind, cold, and wet. There is a temptation to assume that if you are in a warm and dry climate you will need less shelter, or even no shelter at all. However, remember that whatever the temperature during the day, at night it will get cold, and warm areas are subject to changes in the weather just as much as cold areas. In addition, a shelter can provide protection against unforeseen threats and wildlife.

CHOOSING A SITE

Choosing the right site for a shelter is very important. If you select a bad site, you will probably have to build another shelter in a better spot, and will waste valuable time and energy.

The weather can play a key part in determining the location and type of shelter you build. For example, low areas in cold regions have low night temperatures and suffer from windchill. Valley floors invariably have colder temperatures than higher up (these are called "cold air sumps"). Therefore, in cooler areas,

....

Left: Survival shelters can be of almost infinite variety, and range from simple holes scraped out of the earth to large constructions using logs and other materials. The important point is that the shelter matches the conditions.

5

Shelter is the vital physical barrier between you and a hostile outer world.

Making Shelter

Beached

Don't think that shelters have to be complicated. Here a dinghy is converted to a shelter simply by propping it up using the oar, creating a cooling pool of shade beneath.

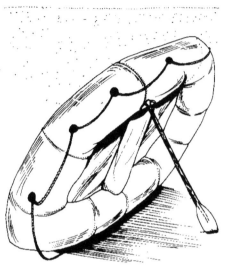

try to situate your shelter where it can take advantage of the sun (if it comes out), and remember to use plenty of insulation material.

In the desert, your shelter must protect you from extremes of both heat and the cold, though dampness will not be a problem. Also consider the following factors:

Wind—In warm areas, locate shelters to take advantage of breezes, but beware of exposing a shelter to blowing sand or dust, both of which can cause injury and damage. In cold regions, choose a site protected from the effects of windchill and drifting snow.

Rain, sleet, and snow—Do not build a shelter in a major drainage route, in a site that is prone to flash floods or mudslides, nor in an avalanche area.

Insects—Build a shelter where there is a breeze or steady wind to reduce the number of insects pestering you. Do not build a shelter near standing water, which attracts mosquitoes, bees, wasps, and hornets, and never erect a shelter on or near an ant hill, unless you want to be bitten and stung.

Sheltering from the weather

Shelters should protect you from the main forces of nature: sun, rain, snow, and wind. Failure to make a shelter dramatically lowers your chances of survival.

Exposure to direct sunlight increases the risk of heatstroke

Exposure to wet and cold increases the risk of hypothermia

SAS TIPS: WHERE NOT TO BUILD A SHELTER

SAS soldiers often have to build shelters quickly when on operations behind enemy lines. They know they must avoid the following spots:

- On a hilltop exposed to wind; it will be cold and windy.
- In a valley bottom or deep hollow; they could be damp and are prone to frost at night.
- On a hillside terrace that holds moisture; they are invariably damp.
- On spurs of land that lead to water; they are often routes to animals' watering places.
- Below a tree that contains a bees' or hornets' nest or dead wood. Dead wood could come crashing down on you in the next high wind.
- Under a solitary tree; it can attract lightning.

Trees—When you are building your shelter, look above you. The tree you are under may contain a bees' or hornets' nest, which you will obviously want to avoid. In addition, look for dead wood in trees above you. In the next storm or high wind, it could come crashing down on you and your shelter.

TYPES OF SHELTER

If you can't find any materials, make use of natural shelters, such as cliff overhangs and gradients. In open areas, sit with your back to the wind and pile your equipment behind you as a windbreak. The following are all examples of natural shelters that can be used by a survivor in an emergency situation:

- Brambles and boughs that sweep down to the ground or are partly broken. Add branches to make them more dense.
- Natural hollows can protect you from the wind. However, be sure to divert the downhill flow of water around your shelter. Use a few strong branches, covered with sticks and turf, as a roof.
- Fallen tree trunks. Scoop out a hollow on the leeward side and cover with boughs to make a roof.
- Stones or small rocks can be used to increase the height of your hollow. To insulate against the wind, plug the gaps between

Undeground shelter

This underground shelter is ideal for use in arid zones. Note how the airspace created in the top of the shelter provides a layer of still-air insulation that protects against the heat of the sun.

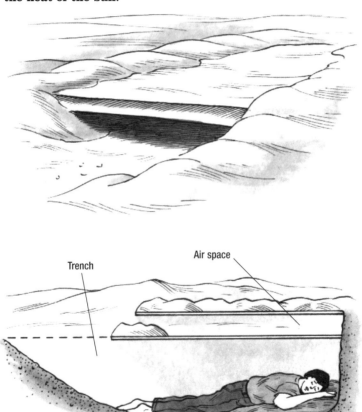

Trench

Air space

Tree shelter

The tree shelter utilizes the trunk of a tree as a robust central support. Fir trees are ideal for this sort of shelter because the canopy of branches forms a natural barrier.

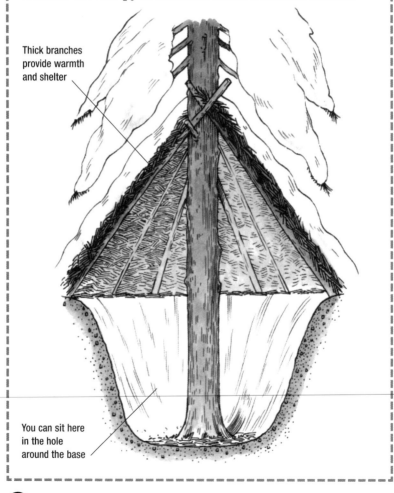

Thick branches provide warmth and shelter

You can sit here in the hole around the base

the stones with turf and foliage mixed with mud.

- Caves can make excellent shelters. If the cave is in a cliff or mountain, you can increase its warmth by building a windbreak over the entrance. You can use stones, rocks, or turf cut like bricks.

If no naturally occurring shelter is available, or you want to create a more permanent or comfortable survival home, then you will need to build your own shelter from scratch. Factors that determine what type of shelter you build are terrain, available natural resources, weather, and snow conditions. DO NOT try to battle with nature: work in harmony with it. For example, if there are trees you can build an A-frame or lean-to shelter; if you are in the Arctic above the tree line, you will want to build a snow cave or snow trench.

General shelters
Tree well shelter
Select a large tree with thick lower branches. Dig out a pit around the tree trunk and make a roof with cut branches and boughs. Lline the walls and floor with the same materials. This is a temporary shelter for use below the tree line. When making this shelter, try not to disturb any snow on the branches.

A-frame shelter
This is a very simple shelter that can be constructed in a relatively short time. You will need the following: one 12 to 18 feet (3.5 to 5.5m) long sturdy ridge pole with all the branches and other projections cut off; two bipod poles 7 feet (2m) long; materials to go over the A-frame or cut branches to form a framework; lashing material.

Lash the two bipod poles together at eye-level height and place the ridge pole (with the large end on the ground) into the bipod formed by the poles, and secure with a square lash (see Chapter 6). The bipod structure should be at an angle of 90° to the ridge pole, with the bipod poles being spread out to an approximate angle of 60°. When you are choosing poles for the framework, ensure that all the rough edges and stubs have been removed. This will ensure that you will not get injured when you are crawling in and out. Once you have built the frame, cover it with a sheet of waterproof fabric or thick layers of branches and foliage. If the latter, start at the bottom and work toward the top of the shelter, with the bottom of each piece overlapping the top of the preceding. This technique, known as "shingling," will let water run off. An extra covering of earth will make the shelter warmer. Make a door plug using a log, backpack, etc.

Lean-to shelter
This shelter is easy to make and can be used in both summer or winter. Build a fire directly in front of it with a

fire reflector on the other side to reflect heat back into the lean-to. When you have built your framework, cover with boughs, using the shingling technique. Remember to insulate the floor.

Willow-frame shelter
This type of shelter is very similar in structure to the A-frame and lean-to. Construct a framework and cover it from the bottom up with boughs. You

A-frame shelter

A-frame shelters are relatively easy to construct, and when properly covered with foliage (plus any other materials, such as a groundsheet) they are warm and weatherproof. If you don't want to make end supports, simply prop the main horizontal branch between two low tree forks.

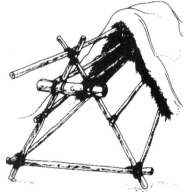

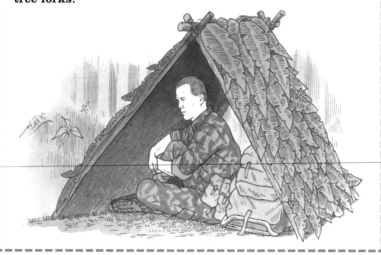

Lean-to

When constructing a lean-to shelter, make sure that the face of the shelter is pointing into the prevailing wind.

can cover the whole shelter with snow in winter.

Arctic Shelters

The need for effective shelter is acute in subzero conditions, and must be part of your immediate action plan if you are thrust into a survival situation in such a climate. Regardless of the type of shelter you build in snow and ice areas, there are a number of principles you must follow in order

Willow-frame shelter

The willow-frame shelter takes some effort and skill to build, but is worth the investment if you are to spend any length of time in the wilderness. Make sure the stakes are firmly embedded in the ground.

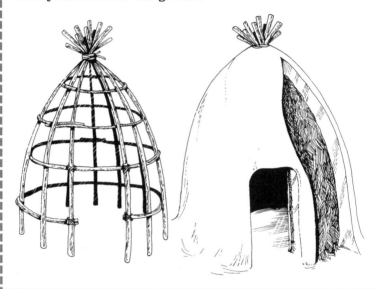

to make your stay in them as comfortable as possible:

Entrances—limit these to save heat. Fuel is often scarce, so keeping entrances sealed will conserve it.

Activity—if you must go outside, make sure you gather fuel, insulating material, and snow or ice for melting. Do not waste your time.

Latrines—relieve yourself indoors when possible. Dig connecting snow caves and use one as a toilet. Failing that, use cans for urinals and snow blocks for solid wastes.

Insulation—always use thick insulation under yourself, even if you have a sleeping bag.

Sleeping bags—keep sleeping bags

Supports

Never build more than you have to. Here two trees provide the supports for a basic shelter.

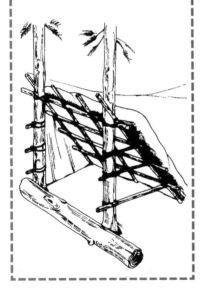

dry, clean, and plumped up. To dry a sleeping bag, turn it inside out, beat out the frost, and warm it in front of a fire. Be careful not to set it on fire.

Snow—brush snow off clothes before entering a shelter. Snow on clothing will melt inside a warm shelter and will turn to ice when the clothing is taken outside. It is better to keep clothing from getting wet than to dry it out later.

Cold—if you are cold during the night, exercise by fluttering your feet up and down or by beating the inside of your sleeping bag with your hands.

The shelters listed below will serve the survivor well in snow and ice regions. Remember to beware of snow accumulating on the roof of your shelter—it may cause the roof to collapse. To make shelters from snow blocks, you will need a saw knife, snow knife, shovel, or machete to cut blocks. The snow from which you cut the blocks should be firm enough to support your weight.

Try to find a place where drifts are deep enough to let you cut blocks from a vertical face (it is less strenuous). It is worth spending time finding snow of an even, firm structure, with no hollow or softer layers. The blocks should be approximately 18 by 20 inches (45 by 50cm) and 4 to 8 inches (10 to 20cm) thick.

Molded dome shelter

This is quick to construct and requires minimal effort. However, you do need some sort of large cloth or poncho with which to build it. Pile up bark or boughs (not too large) and cover the pile with material. Then cover the material with snow (remember to leave a gap for an entrance). When the snow has hardened, remove the brush and cloth. You can make your shelter an entrance block by using a number of small sticks wrapped inside a piece of cloth and then tied off. Remember to insulate the floor of the shelter with green boughs.

Snow cave

A snow cave can be used in open areas where deep and compacted snow is available. Locate the cave on the lee side of a steep ridge or a riverbank, where drifts of snow gather.

Choose the entrance carefully so that wind will not blow into the cave or banks of snowdrifts block it. Burrow a small tunnel into the side of the drift for at least 3ft (1m) and then begin to excavate from this tunnel to both the right and left, so that the length of the chamber is set at right angles to the tunnel entrance.

Molded dome shelter

The advantage of the molded dome shelter is that, unlike an igloo, it requires a minimal amount of skill to construct, and can be done in a hurry.

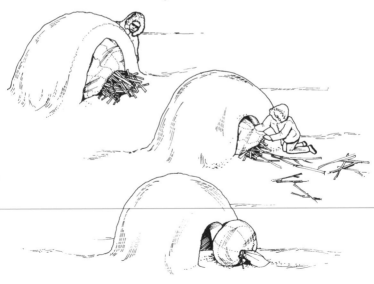

SPETSNAZ TIPS: ARCTIC SHELTERS

Russia's deadly arctic warriors are experts at fighting and surviving in the world's coldest regions. These are their tips for sheltering:

- Do not sleep on bare ground. Use insulating materials such as spruce or pine boughs, dry grass, dried moss, or leaves.
- Do not cut wood that is oversized for your shelter; it uses valuable energy and requires more cord for lashings.
- The superstructure poles must be the largest and strongest because everything else rests on them.
- Do not scatter your equipment on the ground. Keep it in one place to avoid losing it.
- Have a fire going while you are building a shelter. It can be used as a heat source and a morale booster, and can provide boiling water for you to drink later.
- Use clove hitches and finish with square knots for securing boughs together.

The tunnel entrance must give access to the lowest level of the chamber (where cold air collects)—here the cooking is done and equipment is stored. The cave must be high enough to sit up in. It should have an arched roof, partly for strength and partly to ensure that drops of water will run down the sides and not drip on the occupants. The sleeping area is on a higher level than the highest point of the tunnel entrance so that it benefits from warmer air.

The roof has to be at least 1 inch (2.5cm) thick and the entrance should be blocked with a backpack, poncho, or block of snow to retain warmth. Remember to use ground insulation. The cave requires at least two ventilation holes, one in the roof and one in the door. Be especially careful to keep the cave ventilated if you are cooking or heating inside it.

Trench shelter

The trench shelter is a temporary shelter that enables the survivor time to build a more permanent one. Find a large drift of snow at least 3 feet (1m) deep and cut blocks to form a trench just wider

Snow cave

The interior of the snow cave should have a foliage-lined sleeping platform that is higher than the floor. Note also the two ventilation holes bored through the wall of the shelter. Never omit these during the construction.

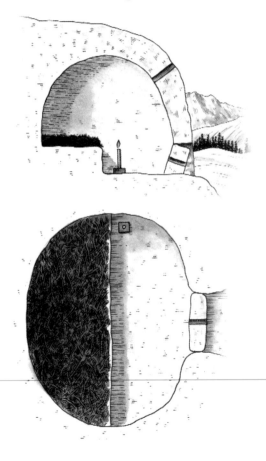

Trench shelter

The trench shelter, like the igloo, is constructed out of blocks of snow. However, because the blocks are cut into rectangular shapes, it is easier to build than an igloo. Remember to line the base of the trench with a thick layer of foliage to protect you from the cold. Hollow the blocks slightly on the inside to form a concave roof.

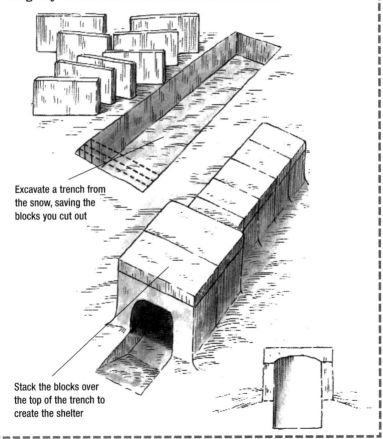

Excavate a trench from the snow, saving the blocks you cut out

Stack the blocks over the top of the trench to create the shelter

U.S. ARMY TIPS:
HEAT AND INSULATION FOR POLAR SHELTERS

U.S. Army personnel are trained to fight in Arctic regions, and part of their training covers the proper construction of shelters.

- If survivors cannot see their breath inside a shelter, it means the temperature inside the shelter is too warm. This will result in dripping and melting.
- To keep breath moisture from wetting sleeping bags, improvise a moisture cloth from a piece of clothing and wrap it around your head to trap your breath inside it.
- Remember that ice reduces the insulating capabilities of a shelter. Therefore, once the inside of a shelter glazes over with ice, chip it off or build a new shelter.
- Check ventilation holes regularly.

than a sleeping bag and long enough to accommodate you. Construct a wall of blocks around the trench and roof it over with large slabs (remember to hollow them slightly on the inside to form an arch). Don't forget a ventilation hole. The trench shelter should not be used over the long term. If you are going to be in the area for a long time, build an igloo.

Igloo

Used by Inuit for centuries, the igloo can be used as a long-term shelter in the polar regions. Draw a circle, about 7 to 10 feet (2.5 to 3m), on the snow to mark the inside diameter of the igloo. Cut snow blocks for the igloo from a trench nearby. When you have around 12 blocks, begin to build. The first row slopes inward with the end joints of each snow block having faces radial to the igloo center.

Next, cut the spiral that will end at the key block. Cut right to left or left to right, whichever suits you. Begin the next layer of blocks, and don't forget to bevel the tops of blocks so the igloo curves inward. When fitting the key block, the hole should be longer than it is wide to permit passing the key block up through and then juggling it into position. Then let the block settle into

Building an igloo

Igloos are difficult for the inexperienced to build, but they are near-perfect shelters for Arctic conditions. The upper faces of the snow blocks should slope evenly in toward the center. The igloo roof is finished with a key block.

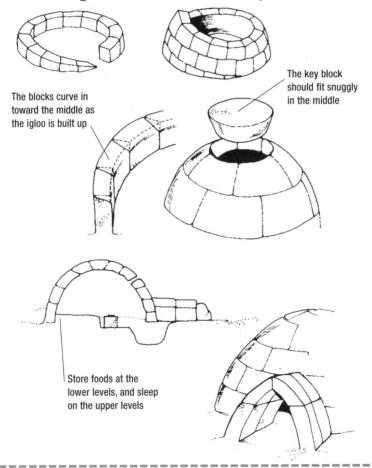

The blocks curve in toward the middle as the igloo is built up

The key block should fit snuggly in the middle

Store foods at the lower levels, and sleep on the upper levels

SIMPLE DESERT SHELTER

If you have a piece of canvas, a poncho, or a parachute-like cloth, you can erect two simple desert shelters. As well as a mound or an outcrop of rock, you will need at least two sticks to support the extended end of the canvas.

Rock method
- Find an outcropped rock.
- Anchor one end of your material on the edge of the outcrop with rocks.
- Extend and anchor the other end to give you the best available shade.

Mound method
- Construct a mound of sand or use the side of a sand dune for one side of the shelter.
- Anchor one end of the material on top of the mound with rocks or weights.
- Extend and anchor the other end of the material to give you shade.

position. Build an entrance tunnel to complete the igloo.

Inside the igloo, you should have a tunnel entrance to trap cold air, a cooking level, and a sleeping level. Put powdery snow on the dome and into open seams: it will harden and be an insulator. You may want to build a windbreak around the igloo to prevent wind erosion. Don't forget to make ventilation holes and put insulating material on the sleeping level. Inside the igloo, all sleeping bags should be placed side by side on the sleeping bench with their head end pointed toward the entrance.

Mountain shelters

Because mountainous areas are predominantly rock, snow, and ice (on the higher slopes at least), there will be few materials available to you for building shelters. Your best bet is to dig into the snow or ice if you have some sort of tool. Build a snow cave if you have some kind of cutting implement. Above all, remember that your number-one priority is to get out of the wind. After that, you should get yourself off the mountain and down into the valleys as quickly as possible.

Desert shelters

Shelter is extremely important in the desert, both to protect you from heat during the day and to keep you warm during the sometimes intense cold of the night. Natural shelters can be

Open shelter

Even though this shelter is open around the sides (something that can be remedied using vegetation, soil, or rocks), the double-sheet construction is ideal for providing protection against hot direct sunlight.

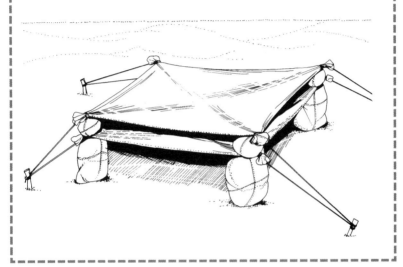

scarce, and limited to the shade of cliffs and the lee sides of hills, dunes, or rock formations.

Caves are good shelters in rocky areas. They are cool and may contain water. However, they can also contain insects and animals, such as rats, mice, snakes, and rabbits. These are all sources of food, and you may be attracted to the idea of having a food store at your fingertips. However, sensible survivors will be

aware of the dangers of bites and stings. Therefore, make sure you stay near the entrance.

When building your shelter, there are three points that you must bear in mind:

- Keep an eye on the weather. If a storm is threatening, avoid gullies, washes, or areas with little vegetation. These are prone to floods and high winds.

- Poisonous snakes, centipedes, and scorpions may be hiding in brush or under rocks.
- Do not make camp at the base of steep slopes or in areas where you run the risk of floods, rockfalls, or heavy winds.

Try to build a shelter that has more than one layer. The resulting airspace will reduce the inside temperature of the shelter. You should place the floor of the shelter about 18 inches (46cm) above or below the desert surface to increase the cooling effect. Try to use a white material as the outer layer of the shelter. The sides of the shelter should be movable to protect you during cold and windy periods and to offer ventilation in the extreme heat.

One more thing: build your shelter to take advantage of a breeze because it will keep you cool and keep insects away.

Desert shelter

This desert shelter is a more basic version of the open shelter shown on page 129. The ground will provide a cooling effect inside. Be careful of snakes and scorpions, however, who will find this type of shelter inviting.

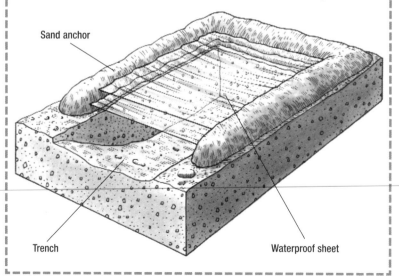

Sand anchor

Trench

Waterproof sheet

Tropical shelters

In tropical jungle and rain forests, the ground is damp and teeming with insects, leeches, and reptiles. You therefore do not want to sleep on it (snakes will be attracted to your body warmth during the night—you may wake up to find one curled around your private parts). Make a raised shelter that allows you to sleep off the ground, and, if you can, you should build a shelter on a knoll or high spot in a clearing well away from standing water, where the ground will be drier, there will be fewer insects, and it will be easier for signaling.

When clearing a site for a shelter, remember to clear underbrush and dead vegetation. Insects and reptiles will be less likely to approach due to lack of cover. A thick bamboo clump or matted canopy of vines will discourage insects and keep the heavy early morning dew off bedding. If you are in a swamp, you will want to build a raised shelter to prevent you from getting wet. Keep on the lookout for four trees clustered in a rectangle and able to support your weight. Cut two poles from any other trees and fasten them to the trees (do not use rotten sticks), and then lay additional poles across them. Cover the top of the frame with broad leaves or grass to form a sleeping surface. When in a swamp, remember to look for tide marks on surrounding trees to ensure you build your shelter high enough.

FRENCH FOREIGN LEGION TIPS: BUILDING DESERT SHELTERS

Knowing when and where to build desert shelters can save you a lot of time and energy. Follow the advice of the French Foreign Legion.

- Build shelters during the early morning, late evening, or at night. It is less physically taxing.
- Try to build a shelter near fuel and water if possible.
- Do not construct shelter at the base of steep slopes or in areas where you risk floods, rock falls, or battering by winds.
- Build shelters away from rocks because these store up heat during the day. You may, however, wish to move to rocky areas during the night to take advantage of the warmth.

The basic jungle-type shelters are the following (see the illustrations for specific examples):

Banana-leaf A-frame

This makes an excellent rain shelter.

131

CANADIAN AIR FORCE TIPS: SHELTERS IN THE JUNGLE

There are a number of simple rules that will help make your stay more comfortable, which you should follow when erecting shelters in the jungle.

- NEVER sleep on the ground: it may be damp and will certainly be crawling with insects.
- Always construct a bed by covering a pile of brush with layers of palm fronds or other broad leaves.
- Do not construct a shelter near a stream or pond, especially during the rainy season: it may get swept away.
- Do not build a shelter under dead trees or under a coconut tree. A falling coconut could kill you.

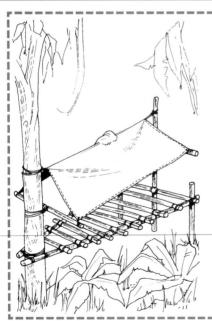

Paraplatform

In tropical areas, build your shelter off the ground, otherwise you will be infested by insects and covered with dew. The poncho strung between two trees will keep the rain off.

Building a raised platform shelter

Platform shelters require a good knowledge of knots and lashings to build effectively. If you struggle with these, try simply propping your base poles between trees and building the platforms on top of these. Illustrated here are two different techniques for constructing the sleeping platforms.

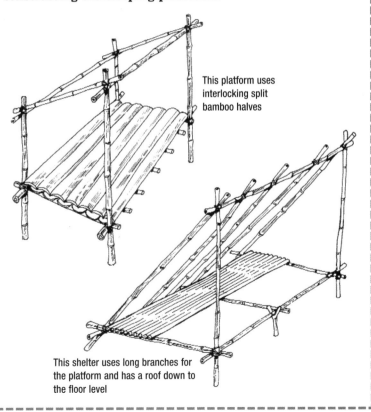

This platform uses interlocking split bamboo halves

This shelter uses long branches for the platform and has a roof down to the floor level

MATERIALS FOR JUNGLE SHELTERS

There is an abundance of shelter-building material in the jungle. Know what it is and how to use it, but also be aware of its dangers.

- Atap, which has barbs at each leaf tip, is a vine that can be used to make shelters. Split each leaf from the tip and layer it on frames.
- Three-lobed leaves can be thatched on a frame.
- Elephant grass is large and can be woven onto a frame.
- Bamboo can be used for pole supports, flooring, roofing, and walls. Be careful when collecting bamboo: it grows in clusters and some stems are under tension. They can fly off and cause serious injury.

Construct an A-type framework and overlap the leaves with a good thickness of broad-leaf plants.

Raised platform shelters
These shelters have many variations.

The poles should be lashed together and crosspieces secured to form the platform on which material mattresses can be made. Try to make the roof waterproof with thatching laid from bottom to top in a thick shingle fashion (it also helps to have a mosquito net). Split bamboo is also very useful for making roofing. Cut the stems in half and lay them alternately to interlock with each other. You can also flatten split bamboo and use it for lining walls or shelving.

Seashore shelter
This shelter can be constructed on tropical coasts, though be aware how far the tide comes in before you build it. Dig into the lee side of a sand dune to protect the shelter from the wind. Clear a level area large enough for you to lie down in and for storing equipment. After the area has been cleared, build a heavy driftwood framework strong enough to support the sand. Then wall the sides and top. You must use strong materials, such as boards or driftwood.

Don't forget to leave a door opening. Cover the entire roof with some sort of material to prevent any sand from sifting through small holes in the walls and roof. This material should be fairly thick and hard-wearing. Cover the roof with 6 to 12 inches (15 to 30cm) of sand to provide insulation.

Covering an A-frame

A basic A-frame shelter can be made in almost any environment and out of any material. Overlap the foliage when covering an A-frame, so any rain runs off downward.

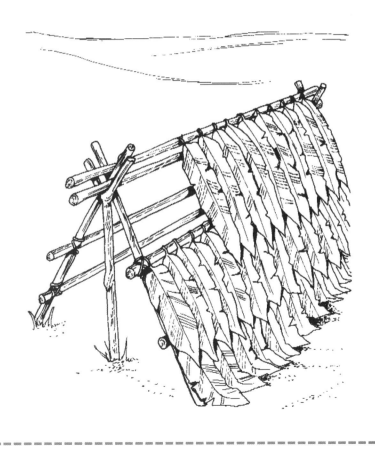

Seashore shelter

The combination of sand and wood used in this construction will make the final shelter extremely durable. With any seashore shelter, make sure that you construct it safely above the high-tide mark to avoid an unexpected flooding.

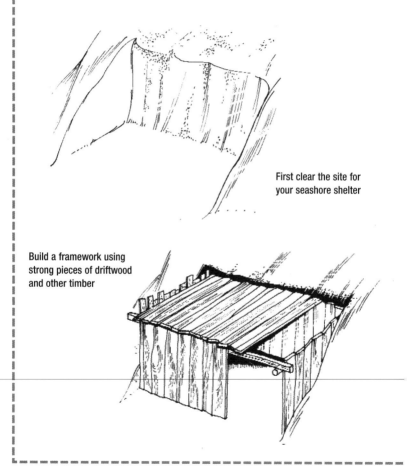

First clear the site for your seashore shelter

Build a framework using strong pieces of driftwood and other timber

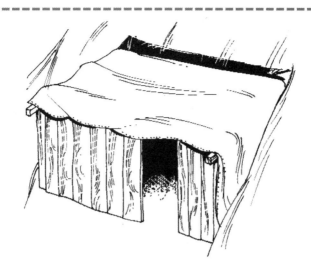

Cover the roof with a piece
of sandproof material

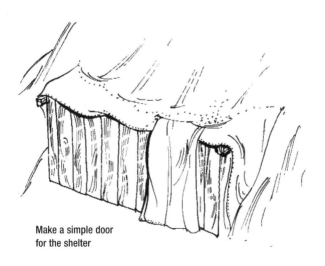

Make a simple door
for the shelter

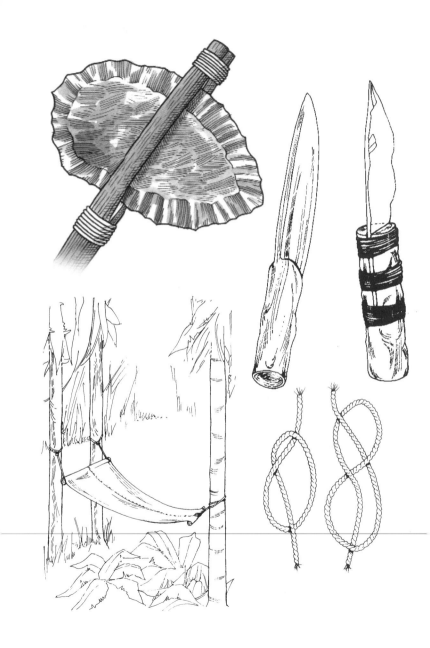

Being able to fashion clothing and tools from the materials around you is a great bonus in a survival situation. Most of what you will make will be simple tools and weapons, but these will make your task of staying alive much easier. In a survival situation, the number of things that you can improvise is limited only by your imagination.

CLOTHING

If you are involved in an air or vehicle crash, try in the short term to salvage as much as you can from the crash site, e.g. towels, tablecloths, drapes, cushions, and seat covers. Almost any type of fabric can be used for bedding, garments, or shelter—be imaginative. You can increase the insulation of your existing clothing by using natural materials. Put dry grass, moss, or leaves from deciduous trees between the individual layers. Paper, feather, animal hair, and down can also be used for insulation.

Waterproof clothing can be made from plastic bags or sheets. In addition, cut off large sections of the bark of birch trees; cut off the outer

6

Camp skills often mean the difference between just surviving and surviving comfortably.

Camp Skills

....

Left: Camp skills refer to a broad range of techniques, from tying ropes to making improvised tools. Remember, however, to use your imagination when it comes to survival, creating survival aids from whatever you find.

Improvised clothing

Scraps of fur and pieces of material can be sewn together to make a rudimentary coat. Pack the coat with insulating materials such as straw or newspaper for extra warmth.

bark and insert the soft and pliable inner bark under the underclothing to protect you from rain. You can also use barks of other trees as long as they are smooth and peel easily.

In terms of footwear, shoe soles can be made from rubber tires. Insert holes around the edges for thongs to tie them over wrapped feet or to sew onto fabric uppers (remember that several layers of wrapping are better on the feet than one). You can also fashion a pair of moccasins from a piece of leather. Place your foot on the leather and cut out a piece 3 inches (8cm) bigger all around than the sole of your foot. Thong in and out around the edges and gather them over wrapped feet. Tie off the gathering thongs and weave another thong back and forth over the foot to make it more secure.

IMPROVISED TOOLS
Club

Despite its simplicity, this is probably one of the most useful tools you can have in a survival situation. It is easy to make and can be replaced with minimal effort. Fashion a club from a branch 2 to 2½ inches (5 to 6cm) in diameter and around 2 feet, 6 inches (75cm) long. It can be used for checking snares and deadfall traps, finishing off a trapped animal, and as a weapon for killing slow-moving game.

CLOTHING TIPS

The uniforms of elite soldiers on extended operations can often wear thin. They are therefore taught how to improvise items of clothing.

- Tie long leaf strips and fibers around a belt or neck band to create a grass skirt or cape.
- Cut a head hole in a blanket or carpet to make a poncho. Tie at waist.
- It is easier to sew together or thong small pieces of hide. Fur on the inside gives better insulation.

Wire saws

Improvise a saw using a green sapling to form a hacksaw frame. You can use the wire saw in your survival tin for the cutting edge. Alternatively, simply insert short wooden handles into the loops on each end of the saw.

Cutlery

Ladles and spoons can be carved from a large piece of wood where a branch attaches—the branch becomes the handle. Look for unusually shaped branches, and make use of these shapes. Where

Saws

The wire saw contained in your survival tin can be fitted to a branch to make a hacksaw (top). Two saws can be used to make an A-frame saw (lower).

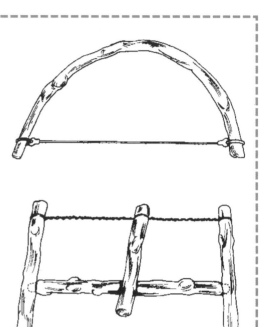

the outline of the object follows the grain, this helps to make it more water-resistant. A simple fork can be shaped from a piece of stick.

Every wood has its unique carving qualities, and with practice you will learn which will best suit your purpose. Sycamore is soft and can be easily carved; beech is a hard wood that is unsuitable for beginners; hazel is a pliable, stringy wood that is easy to carve but tends to split easily; ash is hard to carve, but you should use it for tool handles, bows, and other weapons; birch is a good carving wood but decays easily; yew is very hard and springy and makes fine bows, spoons, and bowls. When you are carving, always be aware of the danger of cutting yourself. Never carve toward yourself, and do not use a dull knife. Do not carve when you are tired, and never carve in a hurry.

Utensils

Wood and bark can be useful aids in a survival situation. Even if you do not want to carve, you can still make utensils from trees and branches. You can use the inner layer of birch bark to construct storage containers or even temporary cooking vessels. The bark can be sewed or tied together, or even glued together using tree sap (which should be allowed to harden).

Bamboo can be fashioned into cups and storage vessels. Cut a section just below a natural joint and then cut below the next joint up. The result is a cup you can drink from, though remember to smooth the

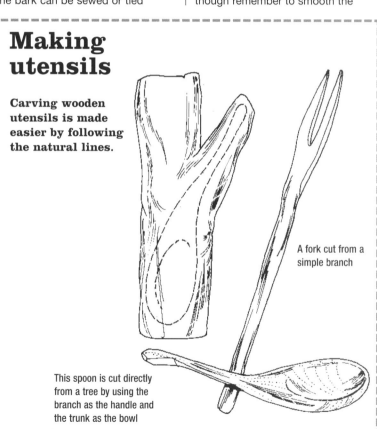

Making utensils

Carving wooden utensils is made easier by following the natural lines.

A fork cut from a simple branch

This spoon is cut directly from a tree by using the branch as the handle and the trunk as the bowl

Bark container

This simple bark container is ideal for storing collected fruits and berries.

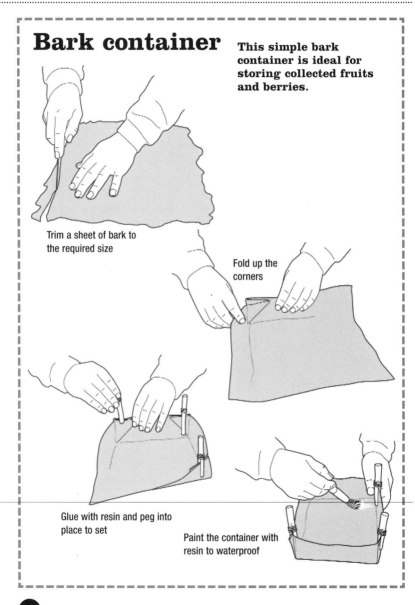

Trim a sheet of bark to the required size

Fold up the corners

Glue with resin and peg into place to set

Paint the container with resin to waterproof

edges to prevent splinters from getting into your lips and mouth.

A forked stick is also a major asset to your camp. Drive one into the ground at an angle of 45° near a fire and rest a longer stick across it. With one end of the stick over the fire and the other driven into the ground and secured with rocks, you can suspend a pot over the fire. Better still, drive two forked sticks into the ground on each side of the fire, rest a straight stick over them, and hang a pot from it over the fire.

Knives

Improvised knives can be made from wood, bone, stone, metal, or even glass. To make a knife from glass,

Making knives

Knives can be improvised from wood (left) and from a piece of metal or glass tied to a handle (right).

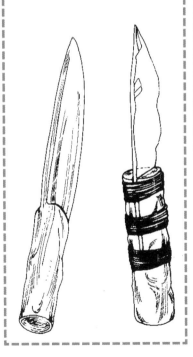

U.S. ARMY TIPS: MAKING A METAL KNIFE

A knife is a vital tool to have if you are a survivor. You should possess one anyway, but if it breaks or you lose it, make another.

- Find a piece of soft iron with a shape that resembles a knife blade.
- Place the metal on a flat, hard surface and hammer it to get the shape you desire.
- Rub the metal on a rough-textured rock to get a cutting edge and point.
- Lash the blade onto a hardwood handle.

simply split a stick at one end, insert a piece of glass, and lash securely. To fashion a knife from a piece of bone, sharpen one end (the leg bone of a deer or other medium-sized animal is best) and fashion a handle from the other end. Even the lids of opened cans of food can be driven into a piece of wood and turned into an improvised knife.

Stone tools

Stones make good hammers either used on their own or lashed to a

Making a stone axe

This survival axe should be used only for light chopping duties, such as breaking up sticks, because the axe head will not be stable enough for heavy applications.

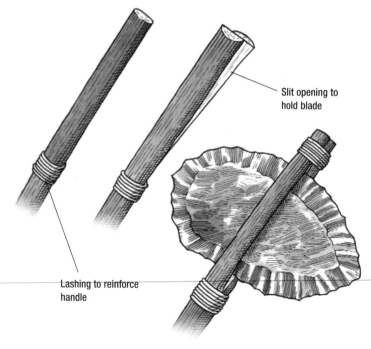

Slit opening to hold blade

Lashing to reinforce handle

handle. Flint, obsidian, quartz, chert, and other glassy stones can be chipped and flaked to make a sharp edge, as a form of improvised knife or scraper. When chipping with another stone, the blow should be made at an angle of less than 90°, otherwise the shock will be absorbed within the stone and the whole stone will fracture.

Bone tools

If you have killed a large animal, do not discard the carcass. Antlers and horns can be used for digging, gouging, and hammering. Using a knife, you can carve a bone, such as a shoulder blade. Split it in half and then cut teeth along it—now you have a saw. Even the bones from small animals can be useful: ribs can be sharpened into points; other bones can be sharpened and the other end burned through with hot wire to produce an eye. The result is a sturdy needle.

ROPES AND KNOTS

It is important for any survivor to have a basic knowledge of ropes and knots. This will be a great help in many situations, such as when building shelters, assembling packs, providing safety devices, improvising tools and weapons, and even for first aid. It is also very important that you practice the knots below before you need them.

U.S. ARMY TIPS: MAKING LASHINGS FROM TENDONS AND RAWHIDE

The U.S. Army teaches its recruits to make lashing material from a dead animal. Tendons and rawhide make excellent lashing materials.

From tendons
- Remove tendons from game the same day it is caught.
- Smash dried tendons into fibers.
- Moisten fibers and twist them into a continuous strand; braid the strands if you require stronger lashing material.

From rawhide
- Skin the animal and remove all fat and meat from the skin.
- Spread out the skin and remove all folds.
- Cut the skin into strips.
- Soak the strips in water for 2–4 hours until soft and pliable.

Ropes

Traditional rope materials include hemp, coconut fiber, Manila hemp, and sisal, but rope can be made from any pliable fibrous material that produces strands of sufficient strength and length.

Many modern ropes are made from nylon or other artificial materials. They are strong, light, and resistant to water, insects, and rot. However, there are drawbacks. They can melt if subjected to heat; they are slippery when wet; and they can snap if subjected to tension over a cliff edge. Remember this when choosing rope.

Rope terminology

Get to know the following words and phrases; they will help you greatly when tying knots:

Bend—used for joining two ropes together or to fasten a rope to a ring or loop.

Bight—a bend or U-shaped curve in a rope.

Hitch—used to tie a rope around a timber or post so it will hold.

Knot—interlacement of ropes or line to form a tie or fastening.

Line—a single thread, string, or cord.

Loop—a fold or doubling of a rope through which another rope can be passed. A temporary loop is made by a knot or a hitch. A permanent loop is made by a splice.

Overhand loop or turn—made when the running end of the rope passes over the standing part.

Reef knot

The reef knot is a simple way of making a secure connection between two ropes, and one that is quick and easy to release.

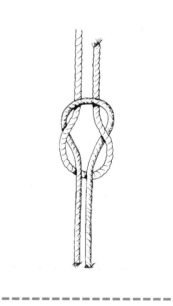

Rope (also called a line)—made of strands of fiber that are twisted or braided together.

Round turn—same as a turn, with the running end leaving the circle in the same general direction as the standing part.

Running end—the free, or working, end of the rope.

Simple knots

The two knots featured here are the overhand knot (left) and the figure-eight knot (right). Most people know the overhand knot, but it can be difficult to untie, especially if wet.

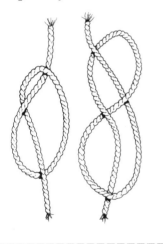

Figure eight

The figure eight is used to make a large, strong knot in the end of a rope.

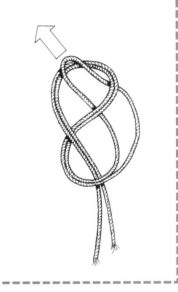

Standing end—the balance of the rope, excluding the running end.

Turn—describes the placing of a rope around a specific object, with the running end continuing in the opposite direction to the standing part.

Underhand turn or loop—made when the running end passes under the standing part.

Knots

There are four basic requirements for knots: they must be easy to tie and untie; they should be easy to tie in the middle of a piece of rope; they can be tied when the rope is under tension, and they can be tied so that the rope will not cut itself when under strain. The following knots fulfill these criteria (consult the corresponding illustrations for further practical guidance on how to tie these knots, and for subsequent loops, hitches, and lashes):

Reef knot

This is the same as the square knot (see below), but it can also be tied by making a bight in the end of one rope and feeding the running end of the other rope through and around this bight. The running end of the second rope is threaded from the standing part of the bight. If the procedure is reversed, the resulting knot will have a running end parallel to each standing part, but the two running ends will not be parallel to each other. This knot is called a "thief knot."

Overhand knot

This is of little use on its own, except to make an end-stop on a rope and to stop the end of a rope from untwisting, but is important because it forms a part of many other knots. Tie by making a loop near the end of the rope and passing the running end through the loop.

Figure eight

This is used to create a larger knot than would be formed by an overhand knot at the end of a rope. It is used at the end of a rope to prevent the ends from slipping through a fastening or loop in another rope. To tie, make a loop in the standing part of the rope and pass

the running end around the standing part back over one side of the loop and down through the loop. Then pull the running end tight.

Square knot

Used for tying two ropes of the same diameter together to prevent slippage. A square knot should not be used for ropes of different diameters nor for nylon rope (it will slip). This knot is good for first aid because it will lie flat against the patient. To tie, lay the running ends of each knot together but pointing in

Fixed loop

The diagram here shows one method of making a strong, fixed loop. The loop can be tied around objects such as logs during the construction of shelters.

opposite directions. The running end of one rope can be passed under the standing part of the other rope. Bring the two running ends up away from the point where they first crossed and cross again. Once each running end is parallel to its own standing part, the two ends can be pulled tight. Bear in mind that each end must come parallel to the standing part of its own rope. A square knot will draw tighter under strain. It can be untied easily by grasping the bends of the two bights and pulling them apart.

Single-sheet bend

Used for tying two ropes of unequal size together. To tie, pass the running end of the smaller rope through a bight in the larger one. The running end should continue around both parts of the larger rope and back under the smaller rope. The running end can then be pulled tight. This knot will draw tight under light loads but may loosen or slip when the tension is released.

Double-sheet bend

This is used for joining together ropes

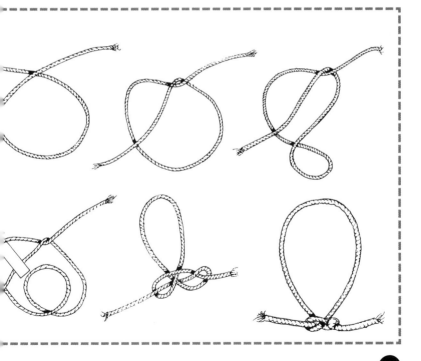

Joining ropes

These techniques are used for joining ropes without creating a significant weak point between the ropes.

Square knot

Single-sheet bend

Double-sheet bend

Carrick bend

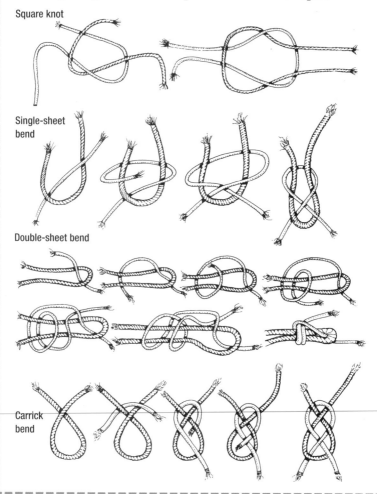

of equal or unequal size, wet ropes, or for tying a rope to an eye. To use, tie a single sheet bend first. However, do not pull the running end tight. One extra turn is taken around both sides of the bight in the larger rope with the running end of the smaller rope. Then tighten the knot. This knot will not slip or draw tight under heavy loads.

Carrick bend

Used for heavy loads and for joining together thin cable or heavy rope. It will not draw tight under a heavy load. To tie the Carrick bend, form a loop in one rope. The running end of the other rope is passed behind the standing part and in front of the running part of the rope in which the loop has been formed. The running end should then be woven under one side of the loop, through the loop over the standing part of its own rope, down through the loop, and under the remaining side of the loop.

Loop making
Bowline

Used to form a loop in the end of a rope. This loop is extremely easy to untie. Easily tied and a knot that will not slip, it can also be tied at the end of the rope by doubling the rope for a short section. To tie, pass the running end of the rope through the object to be fixed to the bowline and form a loop in the standing part of the rope. The running end is then passed through the loop from underneath

U.S. ARMY RANGERS TIPS: THE CARE OF ROPES

America's reconnaissance specialists adhere to the following guidelines when using ropes for their mountain operations.

- Do not step on rope or drag it along the ground.
- Keep away from sharp corners or edges of rock, which can both cut rope.
- Keep rope as dry as possible, and dry it out if it becomes wet, to avoid rotting.
- Do not leave rope knotted or tightly stretched for longer than necessary, and never hang it on nails.
- Exercise care with nylon rope. The heat generated by rope friction can often melt the fibers.
- Inspect rope regularly for frayed or cut spots, mildew, and rot. If such spots are found, the rope should be whipped on both sides of the bad spots (prevented from unraveling) and then cut.
- Never splice climbing ropes.

Loop making

A bowline is one of the most effective loop knots for holding equipment (A); a triple bowline (B) makes a useful sling; a bowline on a bight (C) is a stronger version of the bowline.

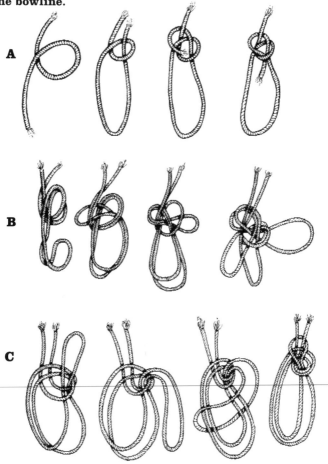

and around the standing part of the rope and back through the loop from the top. The running end passes down through the loop parallel to the rope coming up through the loop. Then pull the knot tight.

Triple bowline

Used as a sling or boatswain's chair (add a small board with notches for a seat). In addition, it can be used as a chest harness or as a full harness. To tie, bend the running end of a line back to approximately 10 feet (3m) along the standing part. The bight is formed as the new running end, and a bowline tied as described for the bowline knot. As a sling, the new running end, or loop (on the right), is used to support the back and the remaining two loops support the legs.

Hitches

Hitches are used for attaching ropes to poles, posts, and bars. Some of the most widely used and useful are given below. Try to master these hitches because they will serve you well in a survival situation.

Half hitch

This is used to tie a rope to a piece of timber or another larger rope. It is, however, not a very secure knot or hitch. To tie, pass the rope around the timber, bringing the running end around the standing part and back under itself.

Timber hitch

Used for moving heavy timber or poles. To tie, turn the running end around itself at least another time. These turns must be taken around the running end itself or the knot will not tighten against the pull.

Timber hitch and half hitch

Used to get a tighter hold on heavy poles for lifting or dragging. To tie, pass the running end around the timber and back under the standing part to form a half hitch (see above). Tie a timber hitch farther along the timber with the running end. The strain is on the half hitch; the timber hitch prevents the half hitch from slipping.

Clove hitch

Used to fasten a rope to a timber, pipe, or post. To tie in the center of the rope, make two turns in the center of the rope close together. Twist them so the two loops lie back-to-back. These two loops are slipped over the timber or pipe to form the knot. To tie a clove hitch at the end of the rope, pass the rope around the timber in two turns so that the first turn crosses the standing part and the running end comes up under itself on the second turn.

Round turn and two half hitches

Used to fasten a rope to a pole, timber, or spar. To tie, pass the running end of the rope around the pole in two complete turns. The

Hitches

Hitches are used when you need to attach a rope to a piece of wood (or similar object) or to another rope. Ensure that the appropriate type of hitch is matched to the nature of the job (see main text).

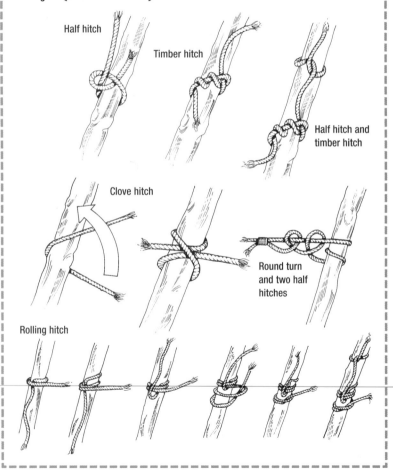

Half hitch

Timber hitch

Half hitch and timber hitch

Clove hitch

Round turn and two half hitches

Rolling hitch

running end is brought around the standing part and back under itself to make a half hitch. Make a second half hitch. For increased security, the running end of the rope should be secured to the standing part.

Rolling hitch

Used to secure a rope to a pole so it will not slip. The standing part of the rope is placed along the pole in the direction opposite to the direction the pole will be moved. Two turns are taken with the running end around the standing part and the pole. Reverse the standing part of the rope so that it is leading off in the direction in which the pole will be moved. Take two turns with the running end. On the second turn around, the running end is passed under the first turn to secure it. To make it secure, tie a half hitch with the standing part of the rope at least 1 foot (33cm) along the rolling hitch.

Lashings

Lashings are used for building shelters, equipment racks, rafts, and other structures. The most commonly used are the square lash, diagonal lash, and shear lash.

Square lash

Used to secure one log at right angles to another log. It is useful for building shelters. Tie a clove hitch around the log immediately under the place where the crosspiece will be located. In laying the turns, the rope goes on the outside of the previous turn around the log. Keep the rope tight. Three or four turns are necessary. Carry the rope over and under both logs in a counterclockwise direction. Make three or four circuits and then make a full turn around a log and a circuit in the opposite direction. Follow with a clove hitch around the same log that the lashing was started on.

Diagonal lash

Used to secure logs at right angles. It is much more effective when the spars do not cross at right angles, or when the spars are under great strain and have to be pulled toward each other to be tied. Tie a clove hitch around the two logs at the point of crossing. Three turns are taken around the two logs. The turns lie beside each other, not on top of each other. Three more turns are made around the two logs, this time crosswise over the previous turns. Pull the turns tight. Two frapping (diagonal) turns are made between the two logs, around the lashing turns. The lashing is finished with a clove hitch around the same pole the lash was started on.

Shear lash

Used for lashing two or more logs together. To tie, place logs side by

Lashings

These lashings are most useful during the construction of shelters (particularly frame-type and platform shelters) and survival rafts.

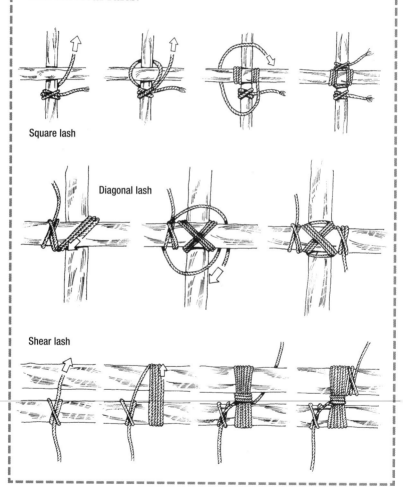

Square lash

Diagonal lash

Shear lash

side. Start the lash with a clove hitch on the outer log. Logs are then lashed together using seven or eight turns of the rope loosely laid beside each other. Make frapping turns between each log. The lashing is finished with a clove hitch on the log opposite where the lash was started.

A shear lash can be used to make a tripod. Get three poles and make turns around all three and frapping in the two gaps. You can then position the bottoms of the poles to make a sturdy tripod. Or, use a shear lash to make an A-frame using two poles secured with a shear lash, though make sure the feet are anchored in or on the ground to stop them from spreading.

It is crucial to check that the poles are secured correctly if they are under strain, and do not forget to check the rope or lashing material regularly for wear.

Hammock

A hammock is an ideal sleeping platform for tropical areas, particularly if protected by a tarp above.

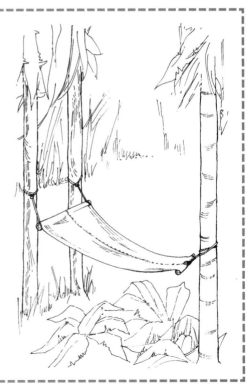

Polar regions, deserts, tropical zones, and mountains present special challenges to any survivor. While temperate zones undoubtedly contain many hazards, extreme climates and terrain can compress such dangers into much shorter time spans. For example, hypothermia can set in within an hour in a polar region if a person is improperly dressed or badly sheltered. This chapter builds on the lessons of previous chapters to explore some of the peculiar challenges of extreme weather and terrain. Remember that temperate zones can experience violent swings in climate, so even if you are not planning to head to exotic regions, you should still read the lessons here. Also bear in mind that lessons concerning shelter in the following environments are contained in Chapter 5, which should be read in tandem with this chapter.

POLAR REGIONS

There are two types of cold-weather areas: snow climates and ice climates. As well as ferocious subzero temperatures, both climates have seasonal extremes of darkness and

....

Left: Extreme climates and terrain present a unique range of challenges. These run from the problems of collecting water in arid tropical zones to the dangers of avalanches in mountainous regions.

7

In extreme wilderness conditions, you must act quickly and decisively to avoid disaster.

Extreme Climates and Terrain

Polar ice cap

The polar ice cap is essentially a landscape formed from a frozen ocean. While the central parts of the ice cap are predictably freezing, the peripheral areas are subject to broad swings in temperature and conditions depending on the time of the year.

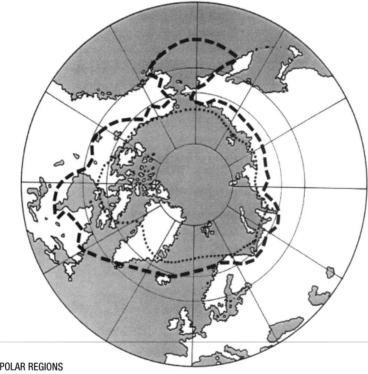

POLAR REGIONS
- - - Southern limit of low Arctic tundra
• • • • • • • Southern limit of high Arctic tundra and polar barrens

daylight. Generally speaking, the nights are long, even continuous, in winter. This can be a problem if you are a survivor: no heat is received directly from the sun and so the temperatures are very cold. The lack of light also restricts the amount of activity you can undertake outside your shelter, though the light from the moon, stars, and auroras reflecting off the white snowy ground does help.

The tree line is the best boundary to define where snow climates end because to the north of it lies the tundra of the frozen wastes. Snow areas are covered by needle-leaf forests, with an abundance of lakes and swamps. The coastlines vary from gentle plains sweeping down to the sea, to steep, rugged cliffs with glaciers at high altitudes. Vegetation ranges from cedar, spruce, fir, and pine trees to dwarf willow, birch, and alder nearer the tundra line.

Regarding ice climates, there are three vast areas of ice on the Earth, which comprise the ice cap regions: Greenland, the Antarctic, and the Arctic. The environment—vast rugged mountains, steep terrain, snow and ice fields, glaciers, and high winds—is harsh in the extreme. There is some stubborn wildlife, such as Arctic birch and shrubs, plus herbaceous plants like grasses, black crowberry, and cowberry. In addition, there are mosses and lichens. All tundra plants are small in stature compared to those that grow in more southerly regions, and they tend to spread along the ground to form large mats. In addition to the incessant cold, the other great threat to survival in all cold climates is the wind. In the Antarctic, winds of up to 110mph (177km/h) have been recorded. The combination of low temperatures and the wind creates a condition known as windchill. For example, a 20mph (32km/h) wind will bring a temperature of 5°F (-14°C) crashing down to -30°F (-34°C). This can pose great danger to the survivor because exposed flesh can freeze in seconds.

Movement

Because of the harshness of the terrain, movement should be undertaken only if your present location is hazardous or if you are near civilization and the possibility of rescue. If you are moving by foot, take only what you can carry. You will burn off a lot of calories and sweat more water than normal (both of which will have to be replaced). If you decide to abandon camp, you must leave some sort of permanent signal to indicate to rescue crews that you have left and the direction in which you headed. The snow block shadow signal (see Chapter 8) is the best signal in snow conditions. It should be as large as possible in an open area and should point exactly in the direction you intend to travel. In addition, you should build further signals along your route so they can be followed.

Making snowshoes

Sharpen the two ends of the stick

Smooth out a long, flexible branch

Tie strong cross mem across the frame as a platform for the foot

Making snowshoes takes some practice to get right, so don't expect the first pair to be perfect. Let each shoe flex a little at the heel and put padding between the straps and your skin.

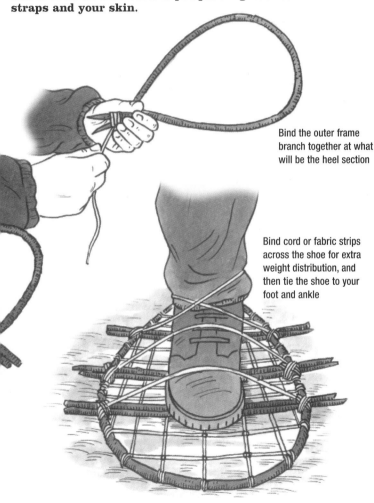

Bind the outer frame branch together at what will be the heel section

Bind cord or fabric strips across the shoe for extra weight distribution, and then tie the shoe to your foot and ankle

SAS TIPS:
NAVIGATION IN POLAR REGIONS

Follow SAS advice and learn to use only reliable navigational aids when traveling in polar regions. Make nature work to your advantage.

- When traveling on sea ice, do not use icebergs or distant sea landmarks to get your bearings. Floe positions can change.
- Avoid icebergs, which have most of their mass below the water. They can turn over without warning, especially with your weight on them.
- Keep clear of sailing close to ice cliffs. Thousands of tons of ice may fall into the sea without warning.
- Migrating wildfowl fly to land in the thaw, and most seabirds fly out to sea during the day and return at night, thereby indicating land.
- Clouds appear black underneath when they are over open water, timber, or snow-free ground, and white over the sea ice and snow fields. New ice produces grayish reflections.

Unfortunately, compasses are unreliable near the poles. Use the stars at night and the shadow-tip method during the day (see Chapter 9). Choose your route carefully at the start of each day. You do not want to get cold and wet by going through swamps and bogs. Try to follow a waterway if possible because most settlements are situated on a river or stream. Also, if you follow a waterway you will be able to replace the fluids you lose through exertion. There will be fish in the river or stream, and animals will be attracted to it to drink,

giving you the opportunity to catch them. In addition, there will probably be an abundance of edible plants growing alongside the water.

When following a waterway, resist the temptation to build a raft and float on it. Many northern rivers are fast, cold, and dangerous and can smash a raft into splinters. You do not know the river, and even if one appears calm, remember that there could be rocks under the water that could tear your raft to pieces. You must also bear the following points in mind when navigating in snow and ice areas:

Rescue procedures

If someone plunges through ice, don't be tempted to go in after them. Remember that the edge of the ice hole will be particularly fragile, so lie down—preferably with someone else holding your ankles—to spread your weight over a wider area. Then extend your hands outward to the trapped person, and pull them to safety.

- Poor roads are of little use for cross-country navigation.
- In winter, long nights, blowing snow, and fog all limit visibility.
- Snowfalls can obliterate tracks and landmarks, thereby increasing navigational mistakes.
- Magnetic disturbances are common, making compass readings unreliable.
- Large-scale maps could be non-existent for the area you are in.
- You may encounter a multitude of lakes, ponds, and creeks that are not shown on your map. This can be confusing and can lengthen travel times.

Clothing and equipment

You should protect your whole body from the cold and wind, especially your head and feet. By keeping active, you will keep the blood circulating in your body, but try not to sweat. If you start to overheat, loosen or remove some clothing. Try to keep your clothing clean—dirt and grease clog the air spaces in your clothing and reduce insulation. Also try to wear goggles. They will stop you getting

CANADIAN AIR FORCE TIPS: POLAR TRAVEL HINTS

Canadian Air Force pilots operate over hostile terrain in the north of their country. If they have to bale out, they must know ice travel skills.

In summer:
- Avoid dense vegetation, rough terrain, insects, soft ground, swamps, and lakes.
- Cross glacier-fed streams in the early morning to avoid raging torrents.
- Travel on ridges and game trails, maintaining constant direction checks.

In winter:
- Do not travel in a blizzard or during extremely cold weather. Set up camp and save your strength.
- Be wary of thin ice, heavy snow, and air pockets if traveling on frozen rivers. Always use a pole to test the ground ahead.

Goggles (1)

A piece of bark with slits for eye holes will protect you from snow blindness.

snow blindness. If you have no sunglasses or goggles, you can make some from strips of thin cardboard, fabric, or even bark with thin strips cut in them for the eyes.

Traveling on foot through snow and ice can be exhausting. Skiing is best on snow with a hard crust, but snow shoes are preferable for deep, loose snow. You can fashion tree branches to make a pair of snow shoes (see illustration). Use willow or any other springy wood, and fashion crosspieces and toe and heel straps. When you walk with the shoes on, the binding should hinge at the toe so you can drag the tail end.

Finally, remember to protect your fingers. Keep your hands covered.

Goggles (2)

Snow/sun googles can even be made from strips of material or camera film.

Do not place them on metal when conditions are extremely cold because you will get a cold burn. If your hands get cold, place them inside your clothing under your armpits, next to your stomach, or in your crotch. Clenching and unclenching your hands in your mittens will also keep them warm.

Finding water and food

The survivor needs a constant supply of food and water to sustain himself in polar regions. In particular, the construction of shelters and signals—even simple movement—results in physical exertion, which in turn increases requirements for food and fluid.

Water

There is an abundance of water in polar regions, in streams, lakes, ponds, snow, and ice. Remember to purify all surface water. If you let the

U.S. ARMY TIPS: ICEBERGS AS A WATER SOURCE

Icebergs, because they are composed of fresh water, offer the survivor a potential source of drinking water in polar regions, but beware. Follow these U.S. Army guidelines:
Exercise caution—even large icebergs can roll over and dump survivors into the sea. This is because most of their mass is below the water, which can be potentially fatal.
Do not drink water obtained from fresh sea ice. Use old sea ice, which is bluish or blackish and shatters easily. This will be free of salt.
Snow and ice may be saturated with salt from blowing spray. If it tastes salty, discard it.

Snow melter

Don't eat unmelted snow or ice. This snow melter consists of a large platform rock with a fire beneath it. The rock is angled downward to direct meltwater into a container.

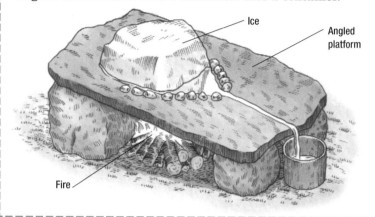

Ice

Angled platform

Fire

water stand, any silt or dirt will settle on the bottom. Do not eat unmelted snow or ice—it lowers the body's temperature, induces dehydration, and causes mild cold injury to legs and mouth membranes. Make a water machine to turn snow and ice into drinking water. Place snow on any porous material, then gather up the edges and suspend it from a support over a container near a fire. The snow will melt and the water will drip from the bag into the container.

Food

In snow and ice areas, there are many types of food, both plant and animal, available. However, you need to know where they can be located and when they are available.

The following Arctic and northern plants should be a part of your diet, especially lichens, which have sustained many survivors here:

Red Spruce Eat the inner bark after boiling and soak the needles in hot water to make tea.

Black Spruce Young shoots can be eaten raw or cooked, and the bark is edible after boiling. Infuse the needles to make tea.

Labrador Tea Use the leaves to make a nutritious tea.

Edible plants

Plant life in the Arctic is very scarce when compared to temperate or tropical zones, though it is not entirely absent. Edible types include Arctic Willow, Bearberry, Black Spruce, Red Spruce, Iceland Moss, Reindeer Moss, Rock Tripe, and Salmonberry.

Common reed

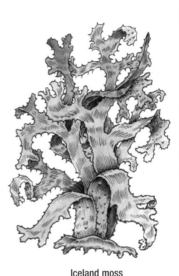

Iceland moss

Arctic Willow The spring shoots, leaves, inner bark, and peeled roots of this plant are all edible.
Salmonberry Berries can be eaten raw.
Bearberry This plant is edible when cooked.

Iceland Moss Soak all parts for several hours and then boil thoroughly to render edible.
Reindeer Moss Soak all parts for several hours, then boil thoroughly.
Rock Tripes Soak all parts for several hours, then boil thoroughly.

Animals

There are many animals that can act as a food source in snow and ice areas, though remember that some of the larger ones can be dangerous and should be avoided unless you have a firearm (see below). If you have a powerful firearm, you can tackle some of the larger species, such as caribou, reindeer, musk ox, and walrus, but be wary of such creatures because all can be dangerous when injured or threatened. (As a general rule, avoid trying to kill bears.) If you are less well armed, creatures that make good eating include: sheep, foxes, arctic hares, lemmings, squirrels, marmots (look for orange-colored lichen on rocks—this indicates their burrows), ducks, wildfowl (these tend to nest or gather around coastal regions or lakes), grouse, ptarmigans, and

Animal food

Arctic animals have the advantages of excellent camouflage and superb senses. A firearm is the ideal hunting weapon for the terrain because it can be difficult to get close to such creatures.

Arctic fox

seals (they are vulnerable when on the ice floes and when they have their young; newborn pups cannot swim and are easy to catch).

Try to preserve some of your meat for future use if you kill a large animal or catch a lot of small ones. Freezing is the best way of preserving fresh meat or fish. Remember to suspend it off the ground, well beyond the reach of scavengers. Always cook meat thoroughly and DO NOT eat the livers of seals or Polar bears because they contain dangerous concentrations of Vitamin A. Remember to bleed, gut, and skin any carcass while it is still warm. Do not eat a diet that consists solely of rabbit or hare. The meat takes more nutrients to digest than it actually provides, meaning that eating it can kill you.

Ice fishing

When lakes are frozen, fish usually congregate in the deepest water. Cut through the ice at this point and bait a hook. Make a pennant from cloth or paper and attach it to a light stick. Tie it firmly at right angles to another stick that is longer than the diameter of the hole in the ice. Fasten the fishing line to the other end of the flag pole and rest the pennant on the side of the hole. When a fish takes the bait, the flag pole will be jerked upright.

Take precautions when using fish as a food source. Do not eat shellfish that are not covered at high tide. Never eat any shellfish that is dead when you find it, or any that do not close tightly when touched. The eggs of the salmon, herring, and freshwater sturgeon are safe to eat, whereas those of the sculpin (which have large shiny heads) are not. In snow and ice areas, the black mussel can be very poisonous. If mussels are

Shrew

Ptarmigan

173

Fish food

While it may be difficult to track and kill polar land animals, fish are often in abundance. Try fishing through holes in ice, using a stick across the hole to hold the line.

Salmon

Barracuda

the only food available, eat only those in deep inlets far out to sea. Remove the black meat and eat only the white meat.

MOUNTAINOUS REGIONS

Mountains can be hostile. Freezing winds, driving snow, ice fields, mist, rain, and sheer drops of hundreds of feet are all potential killers. The survivor must learn how to overcome them all in order to reach civilization. In normal circumstances, mountains and ice fields should be climbed only by experienced and properly equipped mountaineers, and even backpackers should ensure that they have the appropriate professional tools for negotiating snow and ice. However, if you are unexpectedly stranded in mountainous terrain you must know how to avoid the dangers and get safely back to civilization.

Movement

If there is no prospect of immediate rescue, you must get down into the valleys, toward inhabited areas and away from the cold and wet. Do not move in conditions of poor visibility or at night because you could injure yourself. Take the time to survey the entire area around you. Look for a valley—it will probably be the beginning of a small stream or river. Select a safe route to get to it and find a way down. Do not go into avalanche chutes.

If you are on a high ridge, stay away from overhangs—they may break off under your weight. Always try to walk down a spur ridge.

Try not to travel in thigh- or waist-deep snow because you will find it physically exhausting. South- and west-facing slopes offer hard surfaces late in the day after the surface has been exposed to the sun and then been refrozen. East- and north-facing slopes are generally soft and unstable. Slopes darkened by rocks or uprooted trees and vegetation provide more footing. Travel in the early morning after a cold night because snow conditions will be more stable then. The sun can make snow unstable, so aim to travel in shaded areas.

If there are a number of you, move in single file or in echelon formation. When going up a snow slope, traversing (zigzagging) is much easier than going straight up. On snowy

SAS TIPS: UPHILL AND DOWNHILL TRAVEL ACROSS SNOW

SAS soldiers are trained to fight in all types of terrain. Follow their rules for traveling up and down snow slopes on mountains.

- Use zigzag routes to traverse steep slopes: it is less stressful than a straight uphill climb.
- Always rope members of a team together for safety.
- In a team, change the lead person frequently. Since he must choose the route of travel, he will get tired more quickly than the rest.
- When traversing a snow plain, use the heels and not the toes to form a step.
- When going downhill at speed, ensure all items of equipment, especially ice axes, are secured to your packs.

Walking in mountains

Walking in mountains requires constant vigilance and care. Ensure your foothold is secure before you transfer your weight, and don't kick up rocks—they could start a landslide on those below you.

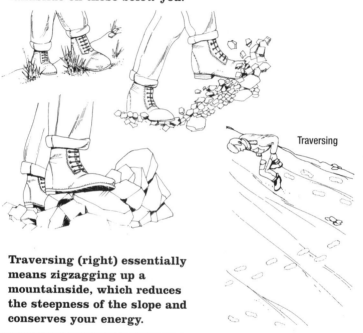

Traversing

Traversing (right) essentially means zigzagging up a mountainside, which reduces the steepness of the slope and conserves your energy.

slopes, stamp in pit steps for solid footing. The steps are made by swinging the entire leg in toward the surface, not just by pushing your boot into the snow. In hard snow, you may need crampons (spiked iron plates that clamp onto your boots), which you should have if you are a backpacker. Space steps evenly and close together to make travel easier and to retain your balance.

When you are descending a snow slope, you can make use of the plunge step or step-by-step descending. The plunge step makes extensive use of the heels and can

SPECIAL FORCES TIPS:
PRINCIPLES OF MOVEMENT ON ROCK OR
STEEP TERRAIN

In mountainous terrain, you must know how to walk correctly. Remember you are in a hostile environment. Follow Royal Marines guidelines.

- Conserve energy: always keep the center of gravity over your feet to make the legs do most of the work, not the arms and upper body.
- Always test holds by tapping the rock and listening for a hollow sound, which indicates instability.
- Keep your hands at shoulder level to ensure blood supply to arms and hands is not reduced.
- Watch where you put your feet.
- Keep three points of contact with the rock at all times.
- Carry out slow rhythmic movements.
- Think ahead. Plan moves and anticipate any difficulties.
- Keep your heels down.
- Remove rings before you start climbing: fingers have been lost because rings have jammed in cracks.

be used on scree (rock piles) as well as snow. The angle at which the heel should enter the surface varies with the surface hardness. On soft snow slopes, do not lean too far forward or you risk lodging your foot in a rut and suffering an injury. On hard snow, your heel will not penetrate the surface unless it has adequate force behind it. If you fail to make sure that your heel enters the snow, you may slip and then begin to slide.

Step-by-step descending is used when the terrain is extremely steep, the snow very deep, or you want to walk at a slower pace. You must face the slope and lower yourself step by step, thrusting the toe of each boot into the snow while maintaining an anchor with an ice axe.

If you are equipped with an ice axe, you can rapidly descend a slope by a method known as glissading. For the sitting glissade, you simply sit in the snow and slide down the

SPECIAL FORCES TIPS:
SHELTERS AND SLEEPING IN MOUNTAINS

Trapped on a mountain? Use the hard-earned experience of special forces soldiers to help you with making shelters and finding a way to sleep comfortably on rocky ground.
- Dig into the snow if there is no shelter among the rocks.
- A plastic bag can make an improvised sleeping bag.
- On a slope, sleep with your head uphill.
- On rough and rocky ground, sleep on your stomach for greater comfort.

Belaying

Belaying is a method of climbing for two or more people using ropes. Note how the rope is anchored to a solid object, and how one person is controlling the rope tension to the climber.

Harness

Tie a rope or tape around your stomach first, wrapping several ties, then bring the rope between the legs and secure with a hitch on both sides of the waist.

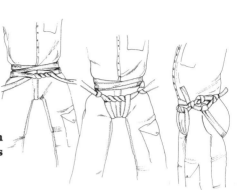

Abseiling

During an abseil, don't lean into the rockface. Instead, lean back at 45°. Wear strong gloves to avoid friction burn.

slope, using an ice axe as a brake. You can increase your speed by lying on your back to spread body weight and lifting your feet into the air. The standing glissade is similar to skiing: position yourself in a semicrouching position with your knees bent as if sitting in a chair. The legs are spread outward for stability, and one foot is advanced slightly to anticipate bumps and ruts. Speed can be increased by bringing the feet close together, reducing weight on the ice axe, and leaning forward until the boot soles are running flat along the surface like short skis.

When glissading, you must bear in mind the following points:

- Only make a glissade when there is a safe runout.
- Never attempt a glissade while wearing crampons: if they snag, you could be thrown down the slope.
- You must wear mittens or gloves to protect your hands and keep control of the ice axe.
- Wear heavy waterproof pants to protect your buttocks.
- Wear gaiters if you have them.

On generally rocky and steep terrain, you should have a rope to assist you. If you don't, descend by facing the cliff on steep faces. On rock faces that are less steep, adopt a sideways position and use the inside hand for support. When ascending, move one foot and hand at a time. Make sure you have a good hold before continuing. Avoid becoming spread-eagled and let your legs do the work. To climb up vertical fissures, use the chimney technique:

Anchor points

Always test anchor points before putting your whole body weight onto them. Watch that your rope isn't cutting into a sharp edge.

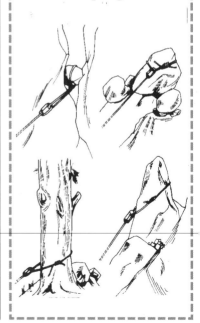

Arresting a fall

When moving through icy terrain, you should always carry an ice axe in case you slip and fall.

As you slide, flip over onto your front and dig the blade of the ice axe hard into the surface.

place your back against one surface and wedge your legs across the gap on the other. Move up slowly. Try to keep good balance when climbing. Remember that it is the feet, not the hands, that should carry the weight. Above all, avoid a spread-eagled position in which you stretch too far and then cannot let go.

Below the snow line, regardless of the type of slope you are on, remember two points: 1) Keep the weight of your body over your feet.

2) The sole of your boot must be placed flat on the ground. Take small steps at a steady pace, and when ascending on hard ground lock your knees with every step to rest the leg muscles. If you encounter steep slopes, remember that traversing is easier than going straight up. Turning at the end of each traverse is done by stepping off in the new direction with the uphill foot. This stops having to cross the feet and risking loss of balance. Take frequent rest stops:

Herringbone step

Walking up a mountainside with the feet pointing outward lessens the stress placed on your ankles.

the ground is more level than on the lower side. When descending, it is best to traverse. Scree slopes are made up of small rocks and gravel that have collected below rock ridges and cliffs. Ascending such slopes is difficult and potentially dangerous. Always kick in with the toe of your upper foot to form a step in the scree. When descending, walk down the slope with your feet in a slightly pigeon-toed position using a short step. Go at a slow pace. On rocky slopes, step on top and on the uphill side of the rocks.

Avalanches

There are a number of factors that cause and affect avalanches. If you know where they are likely to strike, you can hopefully avoid being caught up in them.

Steepness: avalanches occur most commonly on slopes ranging from 30–45°. However, large avalanches can also occur on slopes with an angle of 25–60°.

Profile: slab avalanches, which are the more dangerous kind, have a greater chance of occurring on convex slopes because of the angle and gravitational pull.

Slopes: snow slides in midwinter usually occur on north-facing slopes, which do not receive the sunlight required to stop the snow pack from getting very cold (snow stabilizes better when the temperature is just

you make mistakes when you get tired, which can result in twisted ankles and broken legs.

For narrow stretches of uphill travel, use the herringbone step—ascending with the toes pointed out. When descending, keep your back straight and knees bent, with the weight kept directly over the feet.

On grassy slopes, step on the upper side of each tussock, where

Avalanche protection

This mountainside has numerous features to protect the inhabitants from avalanches. The various fences, walls, wedges, and deflectors serve to break up the strength and momentum of an avalance as it moves.

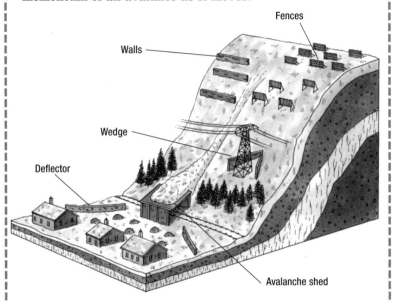

Fences

Walls

Wedge

Deflector

Avalanche shed

above freezing). South-facing slope slides occur most often on sunny, spring days when warmth melts the snow crystals and makes them wet, watery, and heavy. The leeward slopes of a mountain are hazardous because the wind blows snow into well-packed drifts just below the crest. If the surface snow is not attached, a slab avalanche can occur.

Windward slopes generally have less snow and are more compact and therefore usually strong enough to resist any movement. However, they too can be prone to avalanches when subjected to warm temperatures and moisture. Surface features: avalanches are common on smooth, grassy slopes, i.e. those that offer little resistance. Trees and large rocks, on the other

Soft-slab avalanche

A soft-slab avalanche consists of a rapid downrush of powdery snow. Those caught in such avalanches can be suffocated by the volume of snow particles in the air.

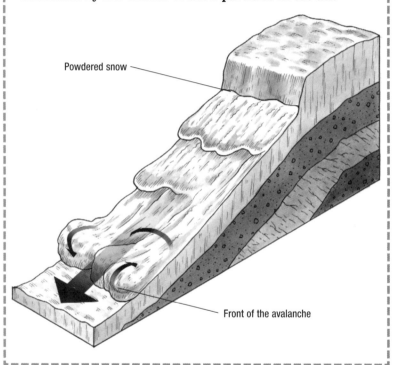

Powdered snow

Front of the avalanche

hand, can bind snow and prevent avalanches from occurring.

Old snow: old snow can cover up natural anchors, such as rocks, causing new snow to slide. A rough, jagged old-snow surface holds new snow better than a smooth surface.

Loose snow: loose snow underneath compacted snow will make a snow slide more likely (there is no rough texture to restrain it). You should always check the underlying snow with a long stick to get an idea if it is loose or compacted.

Hard-slab avalanche

Hard-slab avalanches are particularly destructive. They consist of huge, heavy chunks of icy snow that break off from a sheet and tumble down a mountain at great speed.

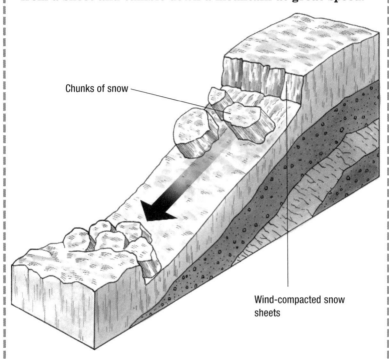

Chunks of snow

Wind-compacted snow sheets

Winds: a wind speed of more than 15mph (25km/h) increases the danger of an avalanche: leeward slopes will collect snow that has been blown from the windward sides.

Storms: a high percentage of avalanches occur after storms.

Snowfall: a heavy snowfall over several days is not as dangerous as a heavy snowfall over a few hours. A slow accumulation lets the snow settle and stabilize, whereas a heavy fall over a short time doesn't give the snow time to settle.

Wet-slab avalanche

A wet-slab avalanche releases large volumes of snow mixed with water, resulting in a dense slab capable of smashing down trees.

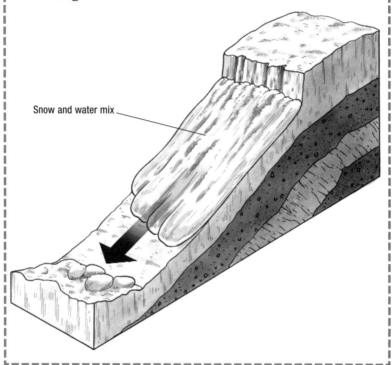

Snow and water mix

Cold temperatures: under very cold temperatures, snow is unstable. Around freezing point, or just above, snow settles and stabilizes quickly. **Extreme temperature differences:** extremes of temperature, especially between day and night, cause adjustments and movement within the snow pack. You must keep alert for any quick temperature changes. **Spring weather:** the sun, rain storms, and warm temperatures associated with spring will cause avalanches, especially on south-facing slopes.

U.S. ARMY RANGERS TIPS: AVALANCHE WARNING SIGNS

Because they operate in mountainous terrain, all U.S. Rangers must have an in-depth knowledge of avalanches and where and when they take place.

- Avalanches usually occur in the same area. After a path has been smoothed, it is easier for another slide to occur. Steep, open gullies, pushed-over trees, and tumbling rocks are signs of slide slopes.
- On leeward slopes, snowballs tumbling downhill or sliding snow indicate an avalanche area.
- If snow sounds hollow, there is a danger of an avalanche.
- If snow cracks and the cracks persist or run, a slab avalanche is imminent.

If you are unfortunate enough to be caught in an avalanche, do the following: Remove your backpack and skis and try to work toward the side of an avalanche. If swimming movements are possible, a double-action back stroke is the most effective, with your back to the force of the avalanche and the head up. Keep your mouth shut: in a powder-snow avalanche, cover your mouth and nose with clothing to form an air space. Save your strength for when the avalanche loses momentum and settles, then try to get to the surface, otherwise your chances of survival are minimal. Try to dig slowly to the surface. If you are in the dark and disorientated, let some spittle dribble out of your mouth—the surface is the

Avalanche survival

If you are caught on the surface of an avalanche, try to "swim" toward the peripheries.

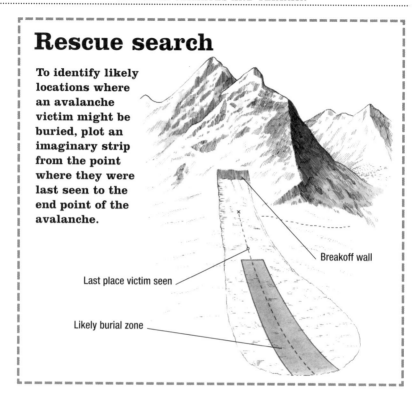

Rescue search

To identify likely locations where an avalanche victim might be buried, plot an imaginary strip from the point where they were last seen to the end point of the avalanche.

Breakoff wall

Last place victim seen

Likely burial zone

---

opposite direction to that in which the spittle runs. Do not panic, but work methodically.

Glaciers

These slow-moving masses of ice can pose multiple hidden threats to the survivor. A glacier is essentially a river of ice that flows at a speed which depends largely on its mass and the slope of its bed. Glacial streams can run just under the surface of the snow or ice, creating weak spots, or they may run on the surface and cause slick ice. Crevasses are often found where a glacier starts at a valley wall, changes direction, or spreads out in a winding valley. They vary in width from a few inches to hundreds of yards. Crevasses tend to be roughly parallel to each other in any given area, and they often develop across a slope. They can be covered with a thin layer of snow and are thus rendered invisible.

Examine a bridge over a crevasse with the utmost caution. If snow obscures the bridge, the lead person should probe the immediate area closely. Be prepared for an arrest or sudden drop. If the bridge is narrow or weak, a team can cross it by slithering on their stomachs, thereby lowering their center of gravity and distributing the weight over a broader area. Where there is doubt about the bridge, but it is the only route available, send across the lightest person first (ensure he or she is securely roped). Everyone should then follow, walking with light steps and taking great care to step exactly in the same tracks.

Bridges vary in strength according to the temperature. In the cold of winter or early morning, the thinnest and most fragile of bridges may have a very high structural strength. However, when the ice crystals melt in warmer afternoon temperatures, even the most sturdy looking bridge may suddenly collapse.

If you decide to jump over a crevasse, make sure that you act as follows:

Ice rescue

If you are on your own and fall through ice into water, try to use any easily accessible spiked objects as picks to steadily lever yourself out of the water. Once you are on flat ice, wriggle some distance on your belly before standing up, to stop the ice from cracking again.

- Decide whether you are going to make a standing jump or a running jump.
- Pack the snow down if you are planning a running jump.
- Locate the precise edge of the crevasse before jumping.
- Remove all bulky clothing and equipment before you jump.

Weather Conditions

Apart from the ever-present dangers of the cold and the wet, the sheer unpredictability of weather conditions on mountains can pose a number of hazards. The weather can change quickly from pleasant sunshine to gloomy skies and driving rain or snowstorms. Mountains cause air currents to be uplifted and disturbed and they attract long periods of severe weather. The wind blows most strongly on mountaintops and across ridges because its speed increases with height. Do not underestimate a strong wind or its

Rain-shadow effect

The windward side of a mountain tends to attract more rain than the opposite side, particularly if it faces the sea. You can use this information either to avoid adverse weather or track down water.

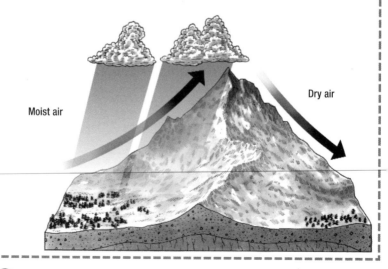

Moist air

Dry air

U.S. ARMY RANGERS TIPS:
GENERAL PRECAUTIONS FOR MOUNTAIN MOVEMENT

In mountainous terrain, U.S. Rangers follow some very simple rules. Study them, and follow the example of America's elite troops.

- Do not kick rocks loose in case they roll downhill—they can be extremely dangerous to anyone below.
- Step over obstacles like rocks and fallen logs to avoid fatigue.
- Do not jump in mountains. Landing areas are invariably small, uneven, and have loose rocks or dirt. You may slip and fall farther than intended.

Cloud types

Generally speaking, the higher and wispier the cloud type, the better the weather. The lower, darker clouds typically signal approaching rain, especially if combined with an increasing wind strength.

Cirrocumulus

Cirrostratus

Altocumulus

Altostratus

Stratocumulus

Cumulonimbus

Nimbostratus

Plant weather indicators

Plants can be good indicators of the approach of rain, usually because parts of them close up as the moisture content of the air increases. The plants here give typical examples of presentations on hot or rainy days.

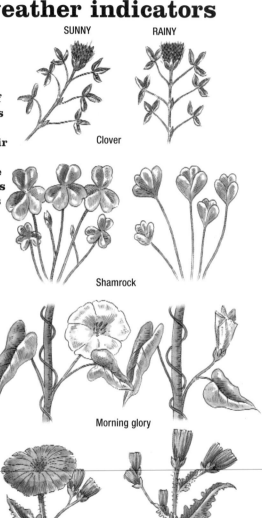

SUNNY

RAINY

Clover

Shamrock

Morning glory

Chicory

chilling effect: it will drain your energy as you try to stay balanced while being buffeted.

The windchill factor is nearly always present in mountainous terrain. Rain tends to be more frequent and heavier in mountainous terrain and can soak you to the skin in a short space of time—be aware of the danger of hypothermia. In addition, you will face reduced visibility due to low cloud, driving rain, mist, whiteouts, or storms, all of which will cause navigation problems for you.

If you have a radio, listen to the general forecasts, or, better still, ring the local meteorological office for a personal weather service. It is very important to give the exact area and time required for the forecast. You should ask for information about the valley and mountaintop weather, temperatures, winds, type of precipitation, visibility, likelihood of a freeze, and any rapid changes

Thunderstorm probability

The combination of a high wet-bulb thermometer reading plus a drop in barometric pressure indicates that a thunderstorm is likely.

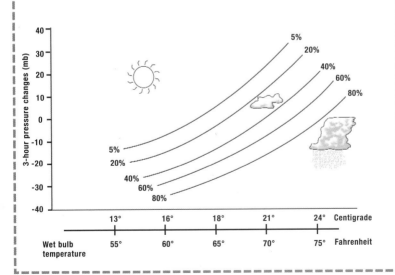

approaching. Obviously you won't be able to do this if you are a survivor, but there is really no excuse for the backpacker to be caught unaware. Remember also that there will be a great deal of local knowledge about the weather. Shepherds, farmers, foresters, and mountain-rescue teams will all know their local area, perhaps even better than weather offices. Always seek their advice before going onto high ground.

Lightning is particularly dangerous in mountains. In a thunderstorm avoid summits, exposed ridges, pinnacles, gullies containing water, and lone trees. Overhangs and recesses in cliffs offer no protection against a discharging current. Leave wet ropes and metal equipment at least 50 feet (15m) from your shelter if possible. Avoid vertical cliffs, which are excellent conductors. Adopt a sitting position with the knees drawn up against the chest. This is the best protection against earth currents.

Finding water and food

There is little food on mountains. You may encounter mountain goats and sheep on the lower slopes, but they are wary and difficult to approach. However, they can be surprised by moving quietly downwind when they are feeding with their heads lowered (remember that they are sure of their footing and you may not be—do not get injured chasing after a mountain

goat). There may also be edible plants on the lower slopes (see Chapter 3). However, your first priority will be to get into the valleys, where there should be ample food. Water is less of a problem on high ground because melted snow, ice, and rainwater collected directly can be drunk without purification.

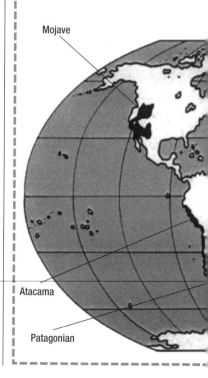

Desert region:

Mojave

Atacama

Patagonian

DESERT SURVIVAL

Deserts occupy around 20 percent of the earth's land surface. The idea that they are all composed of sand is a misconception. There are five types of desert: alkali, sand, rock, rocky plateau, and mountain, but they all share common physical characteristics. You must know what they are so you can prepare your survival plan.

Lack of water

Deserts are characterized by a general absence of water, which is why their human populations are low. Annual rainfall can be zero to 10 inches (25cm), but whatever rainfall

Deserts are found across the globe, with the largest concentrations in North Africa and the Middle East.

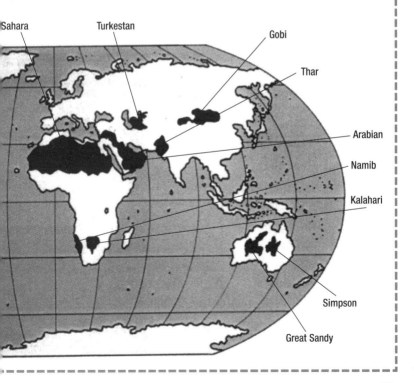

Sahara

Turkestan

Gobi

Thar

Arabian

Namib

Kalahari

Simpson

Great Sandy

Dry riverbed

Dry riverbeds can be useful walking tracks because they may lead to civilization and often contain water beneath the surface.

Water from a dry riverbed

Sometimes water can be sucked up from beneath the surface of a dried-up riverbed by using a tube. Ideally, plug the tube with a porous material to act as a filter.

FRENCH FOREIGN LEGION TIPS: CONSERVING WATER

Water is the most precious commodity in the desert. French Foreign Legionnaires thus implement the following measures to reduce body fluid loss.

- Stay fully clothed and you will perspire a lot less.
- Do not use water for washing unless you have a regular supply.
- Do not rush around. You must keep perspiration down.
- Drink water in small sips, not gulps. If water is critically low, use it only to moisten your lips.
- Keep small pebbles in the mouth or chew grass to relieve thirst.

U.S. MARINE CORPS TIPS: DESERT TRAVEL RULES

Traveling during the day in the desert can be a killer. U.S. Marine Corps regulations are strict concerning movement in desert regions.

- Avoid the midday sun: travel only in the evening, at night, or in the early morning.
- Do not walk aimlessly. Try to head for a coast, a road or path, a water source, or an inhabited location. Try to follow trails.
- Avoid loose sand and rough terrain because they will cause fatigue.
- In sandstorms, lie on your side with your back to the wind, cover your face, and sleep through the storm (Don't worry. You won't get buried.)
- Seek shelter on the leeward side of hills.
- Objects always appear closer than they really are in the desert. Therefore, multiply all your distance estimates by three.

there is, it is usually unpredictable. As a result, flash flooding (where normally dry streambeds are filled with quick-moving flows of water) is common.

Lack of vegetation
Vegetation is generally scarce, and what plant life there is will be specially adapted to withstand the severity of desert conditions. The types present are an indication of the depth of the water table. Therefore palm trees indicate water within 2 to 3 feet (60 to 90cm) of the surface; cottonwood and willow trees suggest it may be found 10 to 12 feet (3 to 3.6m) from the surface. Note: the common sage, greasewood, and cactus have no bearing on the water level and are thus useless as underground water indicators.

Temperature extremes
Desert temperatures vary according to latitude. For example, the Gobi Desert experiences temperatures of -50°F (-10°C) in the winter. On the other hand, the Sahara Desert has recorded temperatures of up to 136°F (58°C). As a result of the unobstructed, direct effect of the sun's rays during the day, temperatures are high, but at night they fall rapidly, especially on elevated plateaus. This is because the surface cools quickly under the clear night skies.

Desert water sources

In a desert, lush green vegetation often indicates the presence of water, such as an oasis. Man-made watering holes may well be nearby.

Dust storms

Winds in the desert can reach hurricane force, generating dense clouds of dust and sand. As well as being extremely uncomfortable physically, visibility is reduced to almost zero.

Mirages

Mirages are the result of light refraction through heated air rising from very hot sandy or stone surfaces. They usually occur when you are looking toward the sun, and tend to distort the shape of objects, especially vertically. During your journey, you may "see" mountains, and lakes that are actually mirages.

Man-made features

All deserts contain at least some man-made features. As a survivor, you should look for them because they may lead to civilization (though the distances may be great). In particular, look out for the following:

Roads and trails: Most road systems have existed for centuries to connect centres of commerce or important religious shrines.

In addition, there are often rudimentary trails for caravans and nomadic tribesmen, and these often have wells or oases every 20 miles (32km) or 40 miles (64km), though in some areas there may be more than 100 miles (160km) between watering places.

Buildings: In the desert, most structures for human habitation are thick-walled and have small

Edible desert plants

These desert plants not only provide decent sustenance, but the prickly pear and the baobab may both contain water, the former in its stem and the latter in its roots.

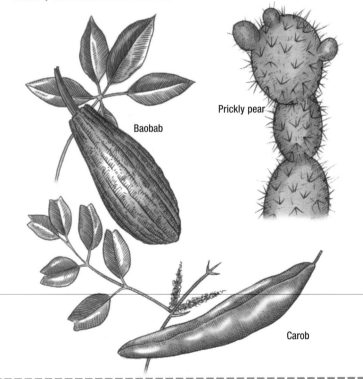

Baobab

Prickly pear

Carob

windows. The ruins of earlier civilizations litter deserts. These can be used as temporary shelters on your journey.

Pipelines: These can lead you to rescue, and because they are often elevated above the desert floor, they can be seen from a long way away.

Agricultural and irrigation canals: These can lead you to people.

Movement

Traveling in the desert can be extremely hazardous. As a survivor, you must consider the effect that the environmental factors, your condition, and the amount of food and water required will have on travel. DO NOT underestimate the climate or the terrain. In daytime, the scorching heat will make movement impractical. However, if you are traveling at night in rocky or mountainous deserts, you may not see eroded drainages and canyons, which could result in you falling and sustaining serious injury.

At night, use the stars and the moon to navigate (see Chapter 8). During the day, use a compass or landmarks. However, be aware that the glare and lack of landmarks in the desert mean that distances are hard to estimate and objects difficult to size. Survivors should try to follow animal trails and hope they lead to rivers or watering holes. The wind can be used as a direction indicator.

CANADIAN AIR FORCE TIPS: IMMEDIATE ACTIONS FOR THE SURVIVOR IN THE DESERT

Deserts are harsh environments—your immediate actions in the aftermath of a crash or being stranded are crucial. Follow Canadian Air Force guidelines:
- Do not walk blindly into the desert.
- Get into shade as quickly as possible.
- Keep your head and the back of your neck covered.
- Evaluate the situation calmly and then decide on a course of action.
- Your immediate priorities are administering first aid if you are injured, and finding shelter and water.

Orient yourself to any prevailing winds once you have established they are consistent and you know in what direction they are blowing. Sandstorms can disorient you. When the storm is over, all the landmarks you were using may be obliterated or

FRENCH FOREIGN LEGION TIPS: RULES FOR DESERT CLOTHING

The French Foreign Legion has more than 100 years' experience of desert fighting. Its men have learned the hard way how to dress for the desert.

- Keep your body well covered during the day.
- Wear pants and a long-sleeved shirt.
- Keep your head covered at all times.
- Wear a cloth neckpiece to protect the back of the neck from the sun.
- Wear clothing loosely.
- Open your clothing only in shaded areas.
- Take off your boots and socks only in the shade.
- Shake your boots before you put them back on in case a scorpion or spider has crawled into one of them.

Headgear

This Arab headdress protects the scalp and neck from heat and the mouth and nose from dust.

Sun goggles

Simple pieces of thin cardboard or bark can be fashioned into sun goggles.

indistinguishable. You must mark your route before a storm so you can pick up the trail afterward. Placing a stick to indicate direction will suffice.

Clothing

Clothing is important in desert areas. You need protection against sunburn, heat, sand, and insects. Do not discard any clothing, and keep your head, legs, and body covered at all times. To stay cool, do not roll up your sleeves but keep them rolled down and loose at the cuffs. Light-colored flowing robes reduce high humidity between the body and the clothing; this helps to keep you cool and limits perspiration. White clothing also reflects sunlight.

Wear sunglasses or goggles if you have them. If not, improvise a pair of sun shades from material or bark. Make the eye slits narrow, and reduce glare reflected from the skin by smearing soot from a fire below the eyes. DO NOT neglect eye protection. Sand and grit can blow into the eyes, causing injury.

Finding water and food

It is vital you find water in the desert. Without water, you will last just two and a half days at a temperature of 120°F (48°C), even if you just rest in the shade. In the same temperature, you will be able to walk only 5 miles (8km) without water before collapsing.

Water in the desert may be underground. Find a dry lake at its lowest part and dig into the ground with a spade, stick, or rock. If you strike wet sand at once, stop digging and let the water seep in. In dry riverbeds, find a bend and dig down on its lower side. If you don't have immediate success, stop digging and find another spot but remember to conserve your energy.

Observe the terrain closely: the likeliest place to find water will be at the base of a hill or canyon. Greenery on canyon walls is an indicator of a seep in the rocks.

Wild gourd

The wild gourd has edible fruit, leaves, and seeds, with water in the stems and roots.

Also look for vegetation, especially reeds, grass, willows, cottonwoods, and palm trees because they usually mark permanent water sources.

Desert plants can be valuable water sources in themselves. Peel off the tough outer bark of a cactus and chew on the liquid-filled inner tissue. The leaf stems of other desert plants, such as pigweed, contain water. Pigweed has fleshy reddish-green leaves and stems. In season, it has yellow flowers and covers the ground in patches.

Food

The U.S. Air Force has a rule: if you have only 1 pint (half a litre) of water

Drawing out a rabbit

Flush out a rabbit from its burrow by making a fire near the entrance to its hole and wafting the smoke inside.

a day, you should not eat at all. Also, you should not eat foods that contain proteins, which require water for digestion, unless you have sufficient supplies of water.

Availability of plant food varies according to geographical area. Date palms are found in most deserts and are cultivated by native peoples around oases and irrigation ditches. Fig trees (straggly trees with leathery evergreen leaves) are found in the deserts of Syria and Europe. Eat the fruits when they are ripe, when they are colored green, red, or black. Learn to identify the following types of edible plants:

Carob—Its seed pods contain a nutritious pulp that can be eaten raw. In addition, its hard brown seeds can be ground and cooked as porridge.

Acacias—The seeds can be roasted and the young leaves and shoots boiled.

Baobabs—The roots can provide water, and the fruits and seeds are edible raw, as are the young leaves after boiling.

Date palms—Fruits and the growing tip of the palm can be eaten raw; the sap from the trunk is rich in sugar and can be boiled down.

Mescals—The stalk is edible after cooking.

Wild gourds—The fruit and leaves are edible after boiling, the seeds after roasting. Chew the stems and shoots for their water.

U.S. GREEN BERETS TIPS: GATHERING AND EATING DESERT INSECTS

The U.S. Green Berets know that insects are a valuable food source. Follow these guidelines and supplement your diet.

- Attract insects at night with a small light.
- Gather crawling insects by lifting up stones.
- The larvae of ants make good eating. Brush them from the undersides of stones into a container of water. The larvae will float to the top.
- Remove the wings and legs of grasshoppers and crickets before eating.
- Always cook grasshoppers before eating.

Prickly pears: The peeled fruits can be eaten raw, the pads must be cooked (cut away the spines). Roast the seeds for flour and tap the stems for water.

All desert grasses are edible. The best part is the whitish tender end that shows when the grass stalk is

205

pulled from the ground; you can also eat grass seeds. Note, however, that flowers which have milky or colored sap are poisonous.

Animal Food

All desert animals, including mammals, birds, reptiles, and insects are edible. You may have to lay traps for the larger animals and birds. However, keep on the lookout for owls, hawks, vultures, and wolves, which often congregate around freshly killed animals. Chase them away and take the meat for yourself. If you are desperate, set a fire in heavy grass or sagebrush: after it has gone out, you can look around for cooked rabbit or rat.

Rabbits and birds can be trapped, but rabbits can be smoked out of their holes by building a fire at the entrance. Be ready to club them when they come out.

Snakes make a tasty meal, but they may be poisonous. You will often find them sunning themselves on rocks and ledges when the sun isn't too hot. (When the sun is at its height, they will stay in shaded areas). They are most active during the early morning or early evening.

Lizards can also be eaten. Look for them under flat stones at dawn, before the sun has warmed the air, and kill them by throwing stones at them or using a catapult. Most people don't like the thought of eating insects, but they can make a tasty and protein-rich meal. However, avoid caterpillars because a few species are poisonous, and stay clear of centipedes and scorpions.

Desert Dangers

Additional threats in the desert come from dangerous animals and plants and also from the various diseases associated with desert areas. However, with a little care and knowledge you can dramatically reduce the risk of such threats.

Dangerous plants

Most desert plants are protected by sharp thorns or spines. The spines have tiny hooks on them that will stick to your skin or clothing if you

Locusts

As unpalatable as they appear to be, locusts are an excellent survival food, providing high levels of protein.

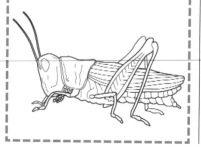

touch them. Give them a wide berth. Poison oak and poison ivy can cause intense skin irritations. Wash your skin thoroughly after exposure to them.

Insects

Avoid ant nests, which can be identified as protruding mounds of soil. If you are bitten, a mudpack will soothe the rash and help to reduce the pain. Also steer clear of centipedes: their bites can be very painful and the effects can last up to two weeks. They hide under rocks during the day and move at night.

Scorpions

Scorpions stay under rocks during the day and move around at night, often into sleeping bags or boots. If you are camping, use a tent with a sewn-in floor. Make sure that you shake out your boots in the morning. There is no real field treatment for scorpion stings, but fortunately, most adult victims of scorpion stings recover, though child fatalities are more common.

Spiders

Spider bites cannot be treated effectively in the wild. You will just have to endure pain, nausea, dizziness, and difficulty in breathing for a few days. It is far better to avoid spiders. Don't allow your curiosity to take you too close to them.

Scorpions

Scorpions love to spend the night in dark enclosed spaces, so give your boots a good shake in the morning before putting them on.

Snakes

Venomous snakes found in desert areas include the cobra, viper, and rattlesnake. Your best protection against snake bites is to wear protective clothing—most bites are below the knee or on the hand or forearm. Do not put your hands into places you cannot see, do not try to catch a snake unless you are certain that you can kill it, and always wear boots. Be careful where you tread.

Lizards

Both the gila monster and beaded lizard (both around 18 inches/45cm long) are poisonous. The gila monster has a large rounded head, thick

Crossing a river

The safest way for a group of three or more people to cross a river is by using a loop of rope as shown. The person who is crossing is either inside the loop or holding onto it, and so can easily be pulled to shore if he or she falls down during the crossing.

chunky body, short stumpy tail, and is brightly patterned yellow. The beaded lizard is darker and larger with a slender tail. Both creatures are docile and will run away from you, so never tease or corner them.

Animal bites

Mammals can carry rabies. Animals in the advanced stage of rabies, especially dogs, will be violent, will stagger, and will foam at the mouth. If you are bitten, immediately scrub the bite area with soap and water and apply disinfectant (if you have it). If a member of your party has rabies and is in the advanced stage, isolate him or her and tie him or her down. Unfortunately, the person will certainly die. Do not touch the body after death. If you are the victim of an unprovoked attack, it is likely that the animal has rabies. Hospital treatment must begin within one or two days to be effective.

Diseases

In the desert, you are vulnerable to many insect-borne diseases, such as malaria, sandfly fever, typhus, and plague. Try to employ preventive medical measures and adequate personal hygiene and sanitation. To prevent intestinal diseases, clean all cooking and eating utensils and protect both food and utensils from flies.

Do not expose your flesh to the elements or to flies; try to wash your feet and body daily; and change your socks regularly. Check yourself for signs of any injury, no matter how slight. Remember that dust and insects can cause infection of minor cuts and scratches. For sanitary reasons, bury all garbage and human waste, but remember to bury them deep because shallow holes can become exposed in areas of shifting sands.

TROPICAL SURVIVAL

The popular image of tropical regions is of thick jungle teeming with danger. In reality, there are different kinds of tropical climates, most of which contain plenty of water, and plant and animal food. The jungle can provide the survivor with everything needed to maintain life: water, food, and a supply of materials for building shelters.

Movement

Before moving on, you should consider your chances of being found and rescued from your present location—you don't want to travel if you don't have to. Food and water should not be a problem where you are because they usually abound in the jungle.

In many cases, rivers, trails, and ridge lines are the easiest routes to follow, though there are some problems associated with them. Rivers and streams can be overgrown, making them difficult

Tropical regions

Tropical regions are concentrated along the equatorial belt, with the largest areas in Central and South America, West Africa, and East Asia.

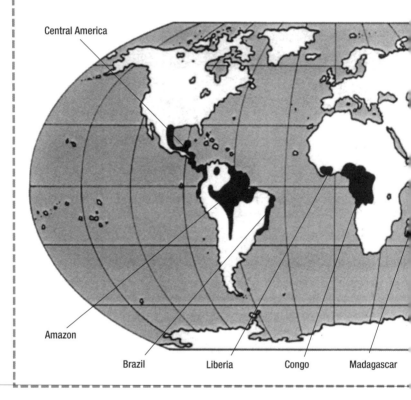

Central America

Amazon

Brazil

Liberia

Congo

Madagascar

to reach and impossible to raft. The waterways themselves may be infested with leeches and dangerous fish and reptiles. Trails can have traps or animal pits on them, and

they can also lead to a dead end or into swamps or thick bush. (One of the best aids to survival in the jungle is a machete. When using it, cut at a down-and-out angle, not flat and

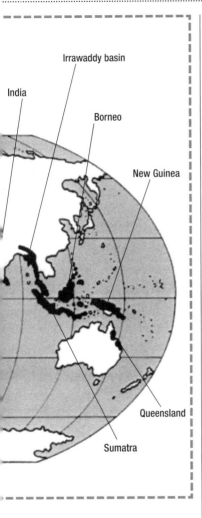

India

Irrawaddy basin

Borneo

New Guinea

Queensland

Sumatra

level—this technique requires less effort.) More hazardous, the vegetation along a ridge may conceal crevices or even extend out past cliff edges.

GENERAL CHARACTERISTICS OF TROPICAL REGIONS

Get to know the nature of the terrain you are in. Tropical regions have a number of common characteristics. Here's a quick checklist:

- High temperatures and oppressive humidity.
- Heavy rainfall, often accompanied by thunder and lightning, which causes rivers to rise rapidly and turns them into raging torrents.
- Hurricanes, cyclones, and typhoons develop over sea areas and rush inland, resulting in tidal waves and devastation.
- There is a "dry" season (during which it rains only once a day) and a monsoon season (when it can rain for days or weeks continuously).
- Tropical day and night are of equal length.

Rattan palm

The rattan palm is a climbing plant that has a creamy white flower as one of its identifiers. Both the stem tips and the palm heart can be eaten, either raw or after roasting.

Despite the hazards involved, waterways often offer the easiest route of travel. If you can, find a stream and travel downstream to a larger body of water. Though following a stream may mean fording water and cutting through dense vegetation, a stream gives you a definite course that will probably lead to some sort of habitation.

It is also a source of food and water and may enable you to travel by raft.

When crossing a stream, look at the opposite bank and ensure that it can be climbed. When selecting a fording site, look for a route that leads across the current at an angle of 45° downstream. Never attempt to ford a stream directly above, or close to, a deep or rapid waterfall or a deep channel.

Avoid rocky places if you can because a fall may injure you (though a rock that breaks the current can be helpful). Remember, deep water need not be a bad thing: it can run more slowly and be safer than shallow water. If you are on your own, use a pole to give you greater balance (drag it in the water on the upstream side), or seek a safer place to cross.

Because darkness falls quickly in the jungle, you must set up camp before sunset. Do not camp too near a stream or pond during the rainy season: flash flooding can erupt without warning. Stay away from dead trees or trees with dead limbs

GREEN BERETS TIPS: MOVING THROUGH THE JUNGLE

U.S. Green Berets are trained to move swiftly and stealthily through the jungle. Follow their advice, and do not make things unnecessarily difficult for yourself.

- Avoid thickets and swamps; move slowly and steadily through dense vegetation.
- Move through the jungle only in daylight.
- Use a stick to part vegetation to reduce the possibility of disturbing ant or scorpion nests with your hands or feet.
- Do not grab brush or vines to help you up slopes or over obstacles: their thorns and spines will cause irritation and they may not hold your weight.
- Do not climb over logs if you can walk around them: you may slip and get injured or step on a snake.
- If using a trail, watch for disturbed areas because they may indicate a trap or pitfall.
- Do not follow a trail that has a rope barrier or grass net across it: it may lead to an animal trap.

Termites

Termites are another type of insect that offers good survival nutrition. These creatures come in several distinct varieties according to their social role (see below). Smash open a termite mound with a rock to gain access.

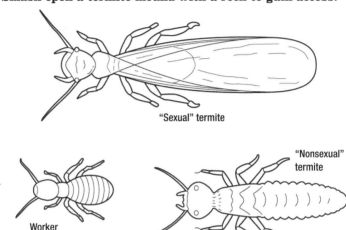

"Sexual" termite

"Nonsexual" termite

Worker

that might fall on you. Be sure to cut away all the underbrush around your campsite to give you room and to allow your fire to ventilate. This practice will reduce insects and hiding places for snakes, and make you more visible to air-rescue craft.

Dangers

Most people assume that the main dangers in the jungle come from snakes and large wild animals. Both are present in tropical jungle areas,

but the main danger to the survivor in the tropics is from insects that transmit diseases or have poisonous bites or stings. Your main adversaries are ticks, mosquitoes, fleas, mites, leeches, spiders, scorpions, centipedes, chiggers, wasps, wild bees, and ants:

Ticks—blood-sucking parasites that can carry infectious diseases and thrive in grassy areas. Brush them off your clothing and check your skin for

Protective clothing

In areas with aggressive biting insects, fashion head protection from netting, improvise gloves, and put elastic bands around cuffs and ankles.

PREVENTING BITES AND STINGS

Insects are perhaps the greatest threat to the health of the survivor in tropical regions. Take the following measures to counter them:

- Use insect repellent, if you have it, on all exposed areas of the skin and on all clothing openings.
- Wear clothing all the time, especially at night.
- Cover your arms and legs. Wear gloves and a mosquito head net if possible to give you extra protection.
- Set up camp well away from swamps.
- Sleep under mosquito netting if you have it. If not, smear mud on your face to keep the insects away.

them at least once a day. If you find some attached to your skin, apply treatment as described in Chapter 9.

Fleas—these are found in dry, dusty shelters. They will burrow under your toenails or skin in order to lay

Dangerous snakes

Tropical areas abound with potentially lethal varieties of snake. Avoid bothering such creatures, however, and they are unlikely to bother you.

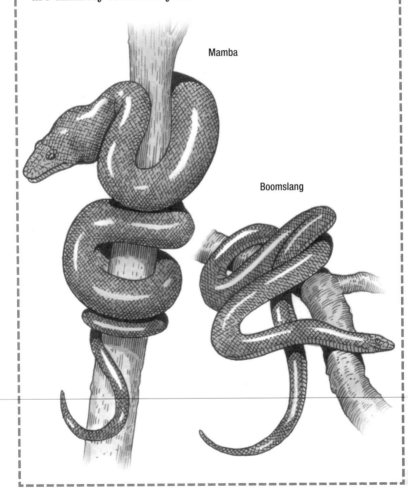

Mamba

Boomslang

their eggs. Remove them with a sterilized knife.

Red mites—carry typhus fever. They burrow into the ground, and are especially common in tall grass and stream banks. Do not lie or sit on the ground, and clear your campsite of as much grass as possible.

Centipedes, scorpions, and spiders—all thrive in the jungle. Scorpions can be found beneath stones and the loose bark of dead trees, but they can also get into shoes left on the ground in the night. Always shake out your shoes, socks, and clothing before putting them on.

Chiggers, wasps, wild bees, and ants—all can harm you through their bites or through transferred diseases. Biting ants live in the branches and foliage of tropical trees, especially the hanging plants attached to mangrove branches. Be careful not to camp near an ant hill or ant trail. Always keep your boots on. Your footwear acts as protection against insects.

Snakes: there are a panoply of venomous snakes in tropical areas, including vipers, cobras, tropical rattlesnakes, mambas, and kraits. Some cobras can spit poison as well as bite. If the poison gets into your eyes or an open cut, wash out immediately with water or, in an emergency, with urine. Under normal

SAS TIPS: SNAKES AND YOUR SAFETY

SAS soldiers are skilled jungle operatives, and know how to deal with the snake threat.

- Be careful where you step: snakes are often sluggish and can be stepped on.
- Some snakes live in trees, so be careful when you pick fruit or part bushes.
- Do not provoke, corner, or pick up a snake.
- Use a stick to turn over stones, not your hands.
- Wear stout boots if you have them. Many snake fangs cannot penetrate boot leather.
- Always check bedding, clothes, and packs before putting them on. Snakes can crawl inside them.
- If you encounter a snake, stay calm and back off. In most cases, the snake will prefer to make an escape.
- To kill a snake, use a long stick and strike it on the back of the head. Make sure you finish it off: a wounded snake is ferocious.

U.S. ARMY TIPS: TOOLS FOR JUNGLE TRAVEL

Movement through the jungle is much easier if you have one or more of the following items of equipment recommended by the U.S. Army.

• A machete to cut through vegetation, collect food and cut logs to make a raft.
• A compass to maintain your direction.
• Medicines to treat fever and infection.
• Boots or sturdy shoes to make walking easier and to protect your feet.
• A hammock to reduce the time needed to make a bed above the jungle floor.
• Mosquito netting to provide protection against insects.

Pigs—all tropical areas contain wild pigs. These pigs have an aggressive nature and are omnivores. They will eat any small animals they can catch, though they feed mainly on roots, tubers, and other vegetable matter. Though they are small—around 15 inches (38cm) high—wild pigs should be treated with caution. It is best to try to kill them with a spear trap.

Do not try to tackle them yourself: their tusks can inflict severe injuries to the legs, which can be dangerously close to the femoral artery on the upper leg. When preparing them for eating, bear in mind that peccaries (a type of wild pig) have musk glands located 4 inches (10cm) up from the tail on the spine. These glands must be removed soon after the animal has been killed, otherwise the flesh will become tainted and unfit for consumption.

Crocodiles and alligators—often lie on banks or float like logs with just their eyes above the water. Be careful when fording deep streams, bathing, or getting near water. Avoid these animals at all times: their tails can inflict a scything blow and their jaws can crush you. If you have to get into the water, move slowly. Thrashing around will attract them.

Leeches—mainly aquatic and are found in freshwater lakes, ponds, and

circumstances, snakes will not usually bother you, but do not handle or provoke any snake and treat all snakes as poisonous. Note: a few tropical snakes, such as the bushmaster and mamba, will attack for no apparent reason.

Wild pig

A wild pig offers a substantial meal if caught. These creatures, however, can be highly aggressive, so should be tackled only if you have powerful weaponry such as a rifle or, at the very least, a first-rate hunting spear or bow.

water holes. They are attracted by disturbances in the water. Land leeches have a large appetite for blood and are easily aroused by a combination of color, odor, light, and temperature. Some leeches living in springs and wells may enter your mouth or nostrils when you are drinking and cause both bleeding and obstruction.

Generally, the bite from leeches is not painful and they will drop off when they have had their fill of blood. If you are covered in them, however, you must take immediate action. You can remove leeches with dabs of salt, alcohol, the burning end of a cigarette, an ember, or a flame. Do not pull them off. If you do, you may pull the head off and leave the jaws in the bite, which may then quickly turn septic.

Fish—be careful in the dry season when water levels are low. South American rivers can contain piranhas, and sharks have been known to attack humans in saltwater estuaries, bays, or lagoons. Barracuda have also been known to attack in murky or clouded waters.

Candiru—a minute Amazonian fish, about 1 inch (2.5cm) long, slender, and almost transparent. It can swim up the urethra of a person urinating in the water, and gets stuck by its dorsal spine. The chances of this happening are remote, but you should not urinate in the water.

In coastal tropical areas, never walk barefoot on coral reefs, which can cut your feet to ribbons. Fine needles from sponges and sea urchins may get into your skin and fester. You may also tread on a stonefish, which will cause agonizing pain, even death. Always use a stick to probe dark holes. Slide your feet along the bottom of muddy or sandy bottoms of rivers and seashores to avoid stepping on stingrays or other sharp-spiked animals.

Finding water

Surface water is available in the tropics in the form of streams, ponds, rivers, and swamps, but you must purify and filter this water. Many plants have hollow portions that collect water. Keep on the

Pitcher plant

The pitcher plant is so called because it catches large amounts of water in the body of its flower. Do not drink it if the water looks stagnant.

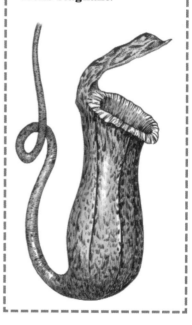

lookout for hollow sections of stems or leaves, Y-shaped plants (palms or air plants), and cracks and hollows. (This water must also be purified.)

Some varieties of vines are water sources, and water can usually be drunk from them without purification (see box on page 225 for qualifications to this rule). When you are drinking from a vine, do not touch the bark with your mouth because it may contain irritants.

Green bamboo

Green bamboo often contains trapped water. Shake the bamboo. If a sloshing sound is heard, it contains water. Cut off the end of a

Bamboo sections

Tap bamboo stems and listen for water sloshing inside. You can then cut out the water-filled section and, if it appears clean, drink the water inside.

Water from a cactus

The interior of a barrel cacti contains water within its pulp. This is accessible by cutting off the top, mashing up the pulp, then drinking up through a straw. Such a process, however, is exhausting, so attempt it only if you have plenty of energy and it is not your only water source.

section that has water in it and drink or pour from the open end, though before you do, look at the inside of the bamboo that contains the water. If the water is clean and white, you can drink it; if it is brown or black or has any discoloration or fungus, you must purify it before drinking. You can also gather water by cutting the top off green bamboo and then bending it and staking it to the ground. Place a container under it to catch the water.

Banana and coconut trees

Banana plants contain drinkable water. Make a banana well out of the plant stump by cutting out and removing the inner section of the stump. Place a leaf from the banana plant over the bowl while it is filling—this prevents contamination by insects and bugs.

Coconuts also contain a refreshing liquid that is safe to drink. The best coconuts to use are green, unripe, and about the size of a grapefruit. The fluid can be drunk in large quantities without harmful effects, though mature coconuts contain amounts of oil, which can cause diarrhea if taken in excess.

Banana tree

Banana trees yield not only edible fruit but also water in the trunk.

Water from a vine

Cut off a section of vine about 5 feet (1.5m) long. Then cut off a short section from the bottom, and drinkable water should begin to drip out.

Food

The jungle is teeming with edible plants and animals. Animals move along game trails in the jungle, and that is where you should place your traps. Among the animals you can hope to trap are hedgehogs, porcupines, deer, anteaters, mice, wild pigs, wild cattle, squirrels, rats, and monkeys.

Reptiles are also abundant in the jungle and should be considered a food source.

If you are near a seashore, fish, crabs, lobsters, crayfish, and octopus can make up a part of your diet—try to spear or catch them before they move off into deep water. Avoid all brilliantly colored or malodorous frogs because these are almost always poisonous.

Edibility test

Before eating any jungle plant, you must put it to the edibility test, unless, of course, you can positively identify it. Citrus fruit trees, yams, coconut palms, papaya, and many other foodstuffs are to be found, but while their are plenty of edible plants in the tropics, masses of poisonous plants also lie in wait for the unwary.

In particular, learn to identify the following poisonous plants before heading off to the tropics: Nettle trees; Strychnine; Physic nut; Cowhage; Duchesnia; Pangi; Castor bean; White mangrove.

AUSTRALIAN SAS TIPS: ENSURING WATER FROM VINES IS SAFE TO DRINK

Australian SAS soldiers are experts in jungle warfare. Use their simple guide to determine whether vine fluids are safe to drink.

- Nick the vine and watch the sap run from the cut.
- If the sap is milky, discard the vine.
- If the sap is not milky, cut out a section of the vine, then hold it vertically and watch the liquid as it flows out.
- If it is clear and colorless, it may be drinkable; if it is milky, it is not.
- Let some of the liquid flow into the palm of your hand and observe it.
- If it doesn't change color, taste it.
- If it tastes like water or is sweet or woody, it should be safe to drink.
- Liquid with a sour or bitter taste should be avoided.

Edible tropical plants

These plants are commonly found in tropical jungle areas. Together they provide many essential vitamins, plus fat and protein in the case of peanuts.

Wild figs

Peanuts

Plantain

Breadfruit

The large, round fruit of the breadfruit can be baked, boiled, or fried for an exceptionally nutritious meal.

Strychnine tree

The Strychnine tree is highly poisonous. Wash yourself thoroughly if any part of your skin comes into contact with any type of poisonous plant.

Wild yam

The tubers of the wild yam are edible, but they need to be thoroughly cooked first to destroy the mild poisons.

Physic nut

Physic nuts might look edible but, in fact, they are one of the tropics' many poisonous plant species.

It is imperative that you can navigate accurately if you decide to move from your camp and head for civilization. In addition, it is important to know how to attract the attention of a search aircraft/party to your position on the ground.

If you are a backpacker, research the area you will be traveling through beforehand, and equip yourself with maps of the area. Study them—they will tell you about prominent terrain features and will enable you to work out viable routes. In addition, always make a note of the wind direction, first and last light, and weather patterns. If you are a survivor, you probably will not have a map, so it is doubly important to know as much about the terrain as possible.

MAPS

Maps contain a wealth of information, which you should learn to interpret so you can make use of it. Maps are available in a variety of scales, such as 1:50000, 1:25,000, and 1:50,000 (it is imperative to choose the one that fits your requirements). The most important map-reading skill is the ability to translate the lines on a map into the actual shape of the terrain.

• •

Left: Signaling and navigation techniques involve a mix of reading nature and using technology. All the techniques require practice to use them with any sort of confidence.

8

In an emergency, your focus should be on attracting rescue or finding your way home.

Signaling and Navigation

Map details

For wilderness adventures, use large-scale maps that include as much geophysical information as possible.

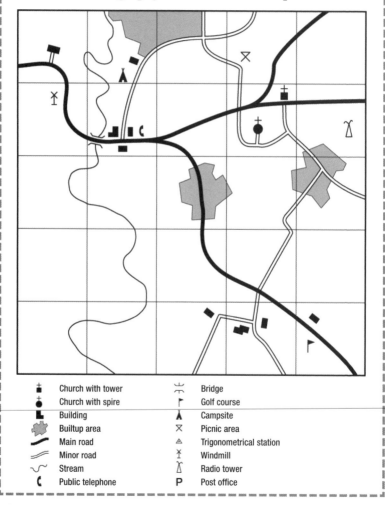

☩	Church with tower	⅂⊤	Bridge
●	Church with spire	⌐	Golf course
◣	Building	⋏	Campsite
❀	Builtup area	⊠	Picnic area
━	Main road	△	Trigonometrical station
⥿	Minor road	⋎	Windmill
⌇	Stream	⋀	Radio tower
(	Public telephone	P	Post office

Grids on maps usually form squares to help you assess distances. You can find a position on a map by quoting grid coordinates. The reference is usually given as a six-digit number. To give readings, always bear in mind that references adhere to the rule "along the corridor, up the stairs." The first three numbers are taken from the bottom or top margin, the second three from the left or right margin (you must mentally divide each map square into tenths to pinpoint the location).

GPS devices

GPS (global positioning system) navigation is an excellent technology for exploring remote parts of the world. It can fail, however, so make sure that you are comfortable with using more traditional methods of navigation.

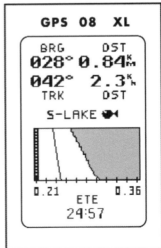

THE THREE NORTHS

The north represented by the grid lines on your map may differ from the north from which you are gaining your physical orientation.

- **True north:** the celestial north that is gained from accurate sun readings or from the stars.
- **Grid north:** the north with which map grid lines are in alignment, and from which map bearings are taken.
- **Magnetic north:** the north to which a compass points, and from which all magnetic land bearings are taken.
- You must be of aware of these variations to take accurate bearings. If you have an adjustable compass and know the extent to which it and your map deviate from true north, you can match them all up to take accurate bearings. You can also find magnetic north using the North Star, the watch method, or the Southern Cross.

Symbols

A knowledge of map symbols, combined with grids, scale, and distance, give enough information for you to locate two points on a map

Contour lines

Shallow gradient

and work out how long it will take you to travel between them.

Contour lines: The undulations and relief of the land are represented on a map by imaginary slices at vertical intervals. By studying these contour lines, you can build up a mental picture of the surfaces and depressions of the land. Contour lines indicate a vertical distance above or below a datum plane. Starting at sea level, each contour line represents an elevation above sea level. The contour interval is the vertical distance between adjacent contour lines (the distance of the contour level will be given in the map margin). Using the contour lines on a map, you can find the elevation of any point and identify terrain features such as hills, valleys, drainage (V-shaped contours), and depressions. The spacing of contour lines also indicates the nature of the slope. Evenly spaced and wide-apart lines indicate a gentle, uniform slope, whereas lines evenly spaced and close together indicate a uniform steep slope. A vertical or near vertical slope is often shown by a ticked contour—the tick always points toward the lower ground.

Bar scales: These are rulers printed on maps on which distances may be measured as actual ground distances. To the right of zero, the scale is marked in full units of measurement and is called the primary scale. The part to the left of zero is divided into tenths of a unit and is called the extension scale. To determine straight-line distances on a

> **Observe map contour lines carefully—the more compressed they are, the steeper the terrain will be for you to negotiate.**

Variable gradient

Steep gradient

map, lay a straight-edged piece of paper on the map so the edge of the paper touches both points. Mark each point on the paper and move the paper down to the bar scale and read the ground distance between the two points.

DIRECTION FINDING

To plan your movements in a survival situation, you must be able to establish where north, south, east, and west are, so you can estimate the direction of travel. This will stop you from getting lost or walking in circles.

Types of compass

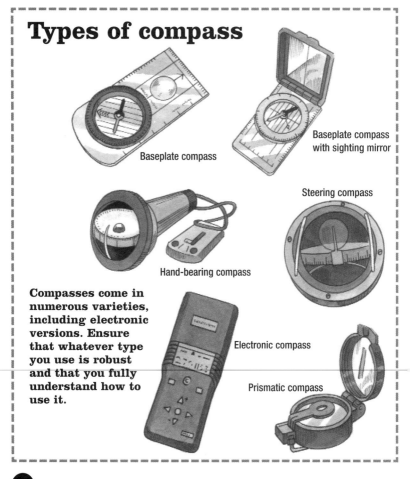

Baseplate compass

Baseplate compass with sighting mirror

Steering compass

Hand-bearing compass

Electronic compass

Prismatic compass

Compasses come in numerous varieties, including electronic versions. Ensure that whatever type you use is robust and that you fully understand how to use it.

Following a compass course

When you follow a compass course, turn your entire body with the compass held out in front of you, so that you and the directional arrow on the compass are both facing on the right bearing.

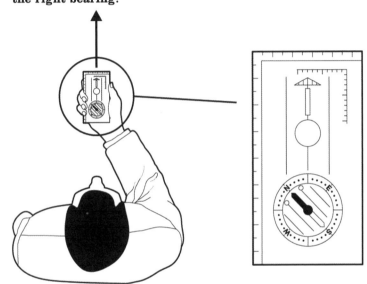

The sun rises in the east and sets in the west, though not exactly in the east and west. In the Northern Hemisphere, the sun will be due south at its highest point in the sky. In the Southern Hemisphere, on the other hand, this midday point will mark due north. The way that shadows move will indicate the hemisphere: clockwise in the north, counterclockwise in the south.

In a survival situation, you can use some simple methods of determining both direction (though they all require the sun): by shadow (see box page 239) and by a watch. However, if you are using a watch you must be wearing one that has minute and hour hands, and not a digital watch. The shadow-tip method is good for spot checks on your journey (it works at any

235

Estimating angles

Estimating angles can be a useful skill for helping calculate distances and also for computing bearings. Some simple hand configurations, shown here, provide rough guidelines to useful angles. Note that every finger's width between sun and horizon represents about 15 minutes of available sunlight.

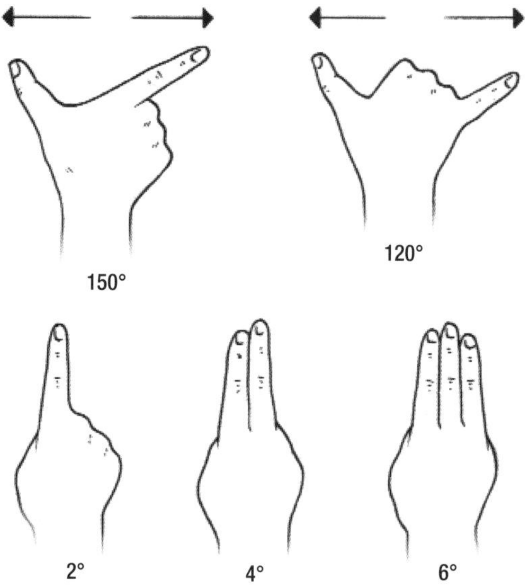

150°

120°

2°

4°

6°

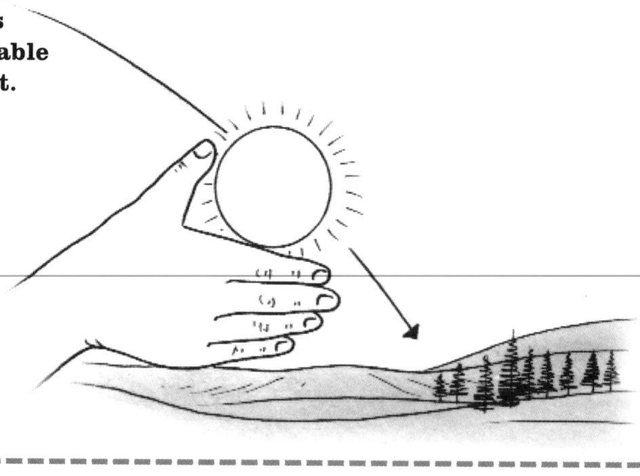

Searching techniques

If you are lost in the wilderness, be aware of how search parties might be looking for you. They will generally use one of the two techniques shown below, while search helicopters will typically describe an ever-widening circle out from your last-seen position.

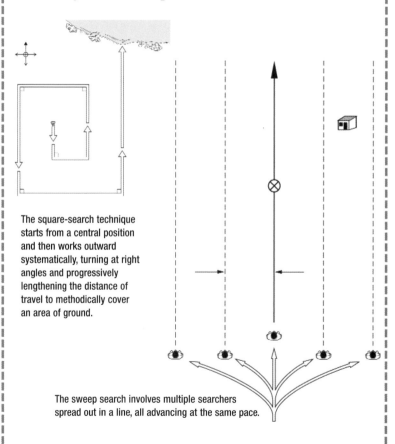

The square-search technique starts from a central position and then works outward systematically, turning at right angles and progressively lengthening the distance of travel to methodically cover an area of ground.

The sweep search involves multiple searchers spread out in a line, all advancing at the same pace.

237

time during the day when the sun is shining).

For watch navigation, use the following techniques. In the Northern Hemisphere, point the hour hand toward the sun. A south line can be found midway between the hour hand and 12:00 hours (if in doubt as to which end of the line is north, always remember that the sun is in the east before noon and in the west in the afternoon). In the Southern Hemisphere, point the 12:00 hours dial toward the sun—exactly halfway between the 12:00 hours dial and the hour hand will be a north line. (It is important to ensure you set your watch to true local time.)

Watch navigation

To navigate by watch in the Northern Hemisphere, point the hour hand at the sun and bisect the angle between it and 12 o'clock to find south. In the Southern Hemisphere, point the 12 o'clock mark at the sun and bisect the angle between the mark and hour hand to find north.

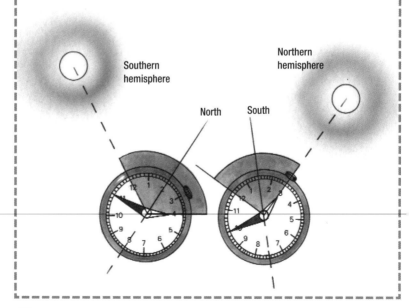

Southern hemisphere

Northern hemisphere

North   South

By shadow

Time-elapse plotting using a shadow can help you ascertain direction (top) and time (bottom).

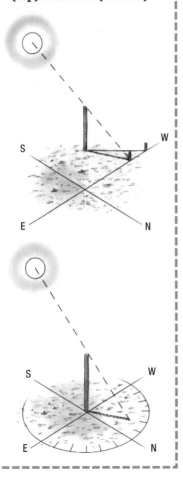

U.S. MARINE CORPS TIPS: DETERMINING DIRECTION BY SHADOW

The United States Marine Corps has a tried-and-tested method for determining location using just a stick and the shadow of the sun.

- Place a stick or branch in the ground at a level spot. Mark the shadow tip with a stone.
- Wait 10–20 minutes until the shadow tip moves a couple of inches. Mark the new position of the shadow tip with a stone.
- Draw a straight line through the two marks to obtain an approximate east–west line (the sun rises in the east and sets in the west—the shadow tip moves in the opposite direction).
- Draw a line at right angles to the east–west line to get an approximate north–south line.
- Inclining the stick does not impair the accuracy of the shadow-tip method, which means you can use it on sloping ground.

The Stars

You can also use star constellations to determine direction. All survivors should know the following information concerning the bearings of stars:

Navigating by the stars

Navigating by the stars has its limitations, especially when cloud cover prevents a clear view of the night sky. Yet when conditions allow, certain stars give very accurate navigational guidance. The following are some of the most easily identifiable stars and constellations.

The Pole Star, North Star, or Polaris (to use its three most popular names) is a sure indicator of north. Extending lines out from the Big Dipper or from Cassiopeia, as shown, will help you correctly identify the North Star, which sits in a relatively isolated aspect in the night sky.

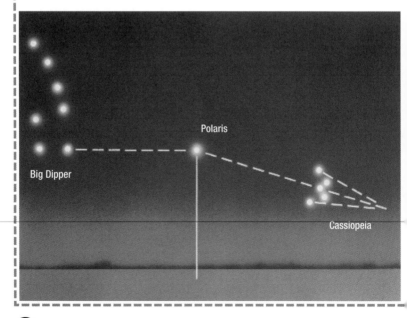

Polaris

Big Dipper

Cassiopeia

Pole Star—in the Northern Hemisphere, this is never more than 1° from the North Celestial Poles (NCP). This is probably one of the most useful stars for determining direction.

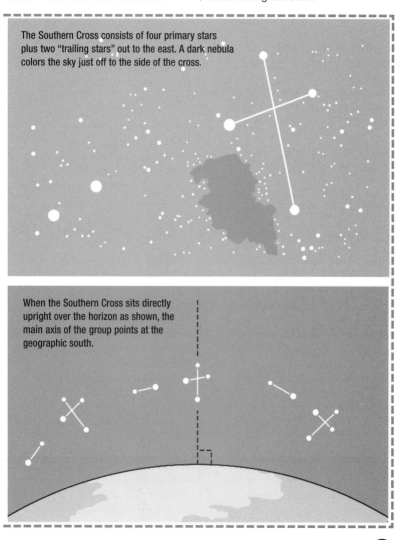

The Southern Cross consists of four primary stars plus two "trailing stars" out to the east. A dark nebula colors the sky just off to the side of the cross.

When the Southern Cross sits directly upright over the horizon as shown, the main axis of the group points at the geographic south.

NAVIGATION AND THE MOON

If the moon rises before the sun sets, the illuminated side will be on the west. However, if it rises after the sun sets, the illuminated side will be on the east. If the moon rises at the same time as the sun sets, it will be full and its position in the sky will be east at 18:00 hours, southeast at 21:00 hours, south at 23:59 hours, southwest at 03:00 hours and west at 06:00 hours.

Big dipper—is very close to the NCP. Its two outer stars point directly to the Pole Star.

Southern Cross—In the Southern Hemisphere, the Southern Cross, a constellation of five stars, can be used to determine south, though unfortunately it is not as easy to find as the Pole Star. To find south, project an imaginary line along the cross and then four-and-a-half times longer beyond it, and drop it vertically down to the horizon.

Coalsack—the dark region in the sky directly above the South Pole.

Orion—rises above the equator and can be seen in both hemispheres. It rises on its side, due east, regardless of the observer's position, and sets due west.

Star movement can also determine your position. If a star is observed over two fixed points for 15 minutes, it will be seen to move. In the Northern Hemisphere, the following rules apply:

- If the star is rising, you will be facing due east.
- If the star is falling, you will be facing due west.
- If the star is looping to the right, you will be facing south.
- If the star is looping to the left, you will be facing north.

Reverse these rules if you are in the Southern Hemisphere.

Natural signposts

If you cannot see the sun, stars, or moon due to weather conditions, you can still determine direction by using natural signposts, though they are not as accurate and you should double check them and treat them with caution. Nevertheless, the following general rules apply:

Trees—normally grow most of their foliage on their sunny side, which in the Northern Hemisphere is the southern side and in the Southern Hemisphere the northern side.

Conifers and willows—usually lean toward their sunny side.

Marking a trail

If you have to move from one position to another, leave trail signs to give search parties or other people information about where you have gone, or to provide details about what lies ahead.

This is the road

Turn left

Turn right

Danger

Bracketing

To avoid getting lost away from your campsite, use the "bracketing" technique. Identify and remember salient features either side of your campsite; that way, you maximize your chances of coming across a recognizable landmark, and can use it to get back to camp.

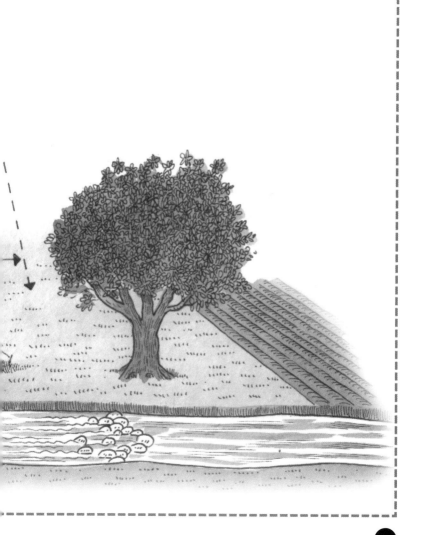

Natural signs

A very rough navigational aid is patterns of moss growth on trees and rocks. Generally, moss likes the darker, cooler north-facing side of objects rather than the hotter, drier south side.

Tracking

Tracking skills involve picking up multiple signs of past movement and putting them together in a direction of travel. Signs change with time. For example, footprints crumble and become full of debris the older they are. The following are good indicators of human/animal presence.

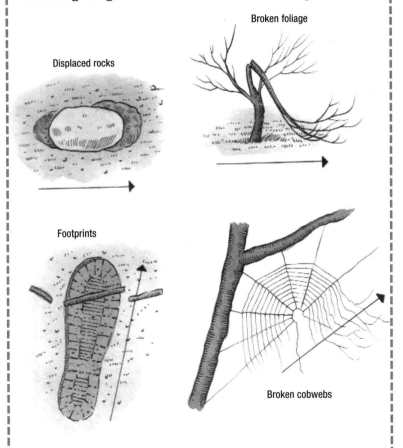

Broken foliage

Displaced rocks

Footprints

Broken cobwebs

Felled trees—their rings are widest on the northern side.

Moss—tends to favor the dark and damp side of its host.

Trees with a grainy bark—these usually have a tighter grain on the north-facing side of the trunk.

Birds and insects—build their nests in the lee of any cover (you must know the direction of the prevailing wind).

Dead reckoning

Dead reckoning is a good way of navigating a route from one location to another, though you will need some sort of writing implement and paper. The method consists of plotting and recording a series of courses before you set out, each one being measured in terms of distance and direction between two points.

These courses lead from the starting point to your ultimate destination, and enable you to determine your position at any time, either by following your plan or by comparing your actual position on the ground in relation to your plotted course.

To navigate by dead reckoning, you will need a number of aids: a map to select your route and for plotting your actual route as you are walking; a compass for direction-finding; a protractor for plotting direction and distance on the map; and a route card and log.

A route card is used to outline the plan of your proposed journey and

A transit

A transit line is useful for keeping a sense of direction when traveling in the wilderness. Plot a straight line on your map between two visible and easily identifiable features. Your relationship to this line will give you constant feedback about whether you are still on the right course of travel.

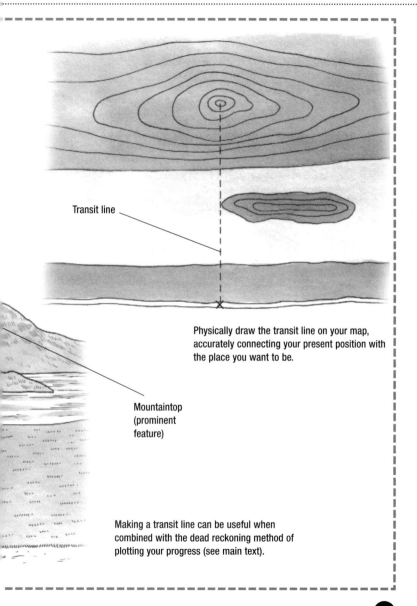

Transit line

Physically draw the transit line on your map, accurately connecting your present position with the place you want to be.

Mountaintop (prominent feature)

Making a transit line can be useful when combined with the dead reckoning method of plotting your progress (see main text).

the log is used to record the distance you have actually traveled.

Having determined your starting point and plotted your route on the map, make out your route card. This describes each leg of the proposed route in terms of distance and direction. When you have completed your route card, you are ready to move. When you are walking, keep a

Maps and the landscape

When reading a map, mentally interpret what three-dimensional information it is giving, and so avoid picking hard or hazardous routes.

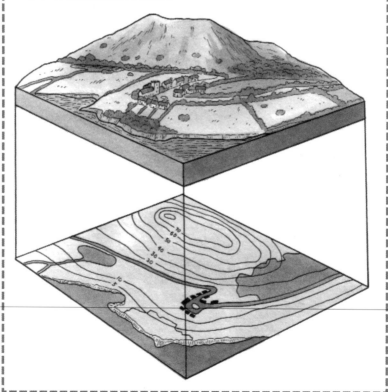

Map grid

When giving a six-digit map reading, take your first reading from the top or bottom margin, and your second reading from the left- or right-hand margin. The map reference here is 20.4 x 55.8.

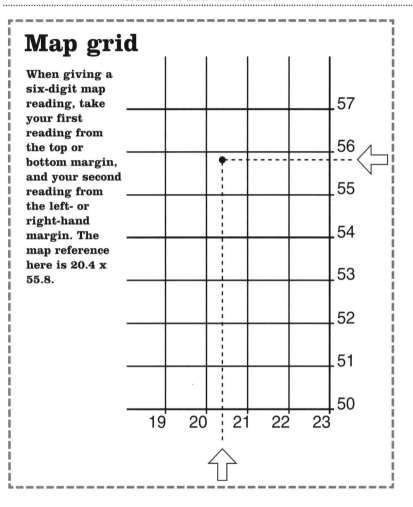

careful record of each bearing taken and the distance covered on each bearing. This record is your log— your memory is not enough. If you have to deviate from your route because of terrain, then you must

make adjustments to your route and record them in the log.

When using dead reckoning, it is important to establish the length of your average pace. However, when you are computing your average pace, remember to take into account the following:

Slopes: the pace lengthens on a downward slope and shortens on an upward slope, though not too much on very gentle slopes.

Winds: a headwind shortens the pace and a tailwind increases it.

Surfaces: gravel, mud, sand, long grass, deep snow, and similar surface materials tend to shorten the pace.

Elements: snow, rain, and ice all reduce the length of the pace.

Clothing: carrying excess weight of clothing shortens the pace and your shoe type can affect traction and therefore your pace length.

SIGNALING

As a survivor, it is important that you are able to give signals which a rescue team, specifically an aircraft, will be able to see clearly. You must plan your signaling system early on so that you know how to use it and can do so at short notice.

Unless you have a radio or flares, smoke and fire are your best ways to alert a rescue aircraft. If you are a backpacker, it is also a good idea to

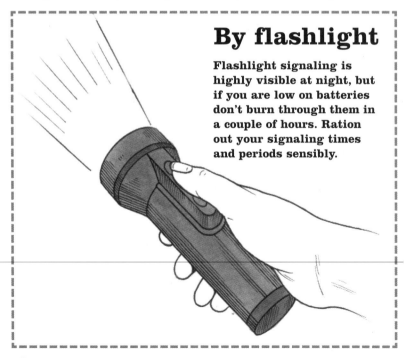

By flashlight

Flashlight signaling is highly visible at night, but if you are low on batteries don't burn through them in a couple of hours. Ration out your signaling times and periods sensibly.

equip yourself with some of the items listed below:

Transceiver: can transmit tone or voice and will also receive tone or voice.

Beacon: can only transmit tone.

Radio: survival radios are generally line-of-sight communication devices, so the best transmission range will be obtained when you are operating from clear, unobstructed terrain.

Hand-held flares: day flares produce a brightly colored smoke; night

Whistle

Easy to carry, a whistle is one of the most useful tools for short-range contact.

Radio

A simple VHF radio will give you good short-range communications, and will operate where cell phones lose their connection with satellites.

flares are very bright and can be seen over long distances.

Hand-held launched flares: these overcome the problems of terrain masking and climatic conditions.

Tracer ammunition: if available, use it for signaling. When fired, the round appears as an orange-red flash. Do not direct it at a rescue aircraft.

Sea marker: a rapid dispersion powder that stains the sea green or orange.

Paulin signals: rubberized nylon markers that are blue on one side and yellow on the other.

Whistle: good for short-range signaling.

Light signals: flashlights or strobe lights can be seen over great distances.

If professionally produced signaling equipment is not available to you, however, you will have to improvise, using smoke or fire, or simply ground-to-air signals.

SPECIAL FORCES TIPS: SIGNAL FIRES

Learn these special forces tips about where to build signal fires. You must get it right the first time—you may not get a second chance.

- Keep green boughs, oil, or rubber close by to create smoke.
- Build earth wells around fires if surrounded by vegetation or trees.
- Build fires in clearings. Do not build among trees: the canopy will block out the signal.
- If by a river or lake, build rafts to place fires on and anchor or tether them in position.

Flares

Hold your flare at arms length, and keep the flare downwind so that the smoke and flame do not blow across you.

Signaling with a mirror

Mirror signaling projects bursts of vivid light over many miles, and can be performed with materials ranging from polished metal to DVDs/CDs.

Improvising

Large pieces of colored material are ideal for attracting attention at sea or on land.

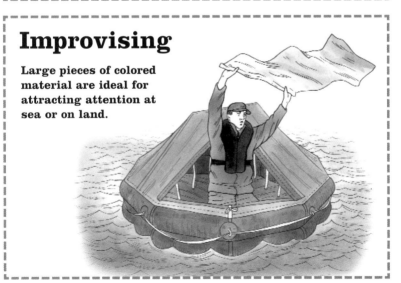

Ground-to air-signals

Make these signals large, bold, and with contrasting materials to provide information about your situation to overflying aircraft.

Need doctor

Need medical supplies

Unable to proceed

Require food and water

Need firearms

Need map/compass

Need signal lamp

Indicates direction to proceed

Am moving this direction

Will try to take off

Aircraft damaged

Safe to land

Need fuel/oil

All is well

No

Yes

Not understood

Require engineer

Smoke

In daylight, smoke is recognizable over long distances. Signal fires should be built, covered, and maintained, ready to be lit at a moment's notice. You can create smoke that will contrast with the background terrain: green leaves, moss, or damp wood on a fire produce white smoke; rubber or oil-soaked rags on a fire produce black smoke. To build a smoke generator, make a large log cabin fire (see Chapter 4) on the ground. This provides excellent ventilation and supports the green boughs used for producing the smoke. Place smoke-producing materials over the fire and ignite the fire when an aircraft is in the immediate vicinity. If you are in snow or ice terrain, build the fire on a raised platform above the wet ground, or it will burn through the snow.

Fire

A blazing fire is very effective for signaling at night, so build a fire that gives out a lot of light. In an emergency, a burning tree is a good way of attracting attention—pitch-bearing trees can be set on fire when green. For other types of trees, place dry wood in the lower branches, and set it on fire. Remember to select a tree apart from other trees—you do not want to start a forest fire.

U.S. ARMY TIPS: SIGNALS USING NATURAL MATERIALS

If you become stranded in the wild, follow U.S. Army advice and construct signals from the materials around you.

- Build brush or snow mounds that will cast shadows.
- In snow, tramp down the snow to form letters or symbols and fill in with contrasting materials: twigs or branches.
- In sand, use boulders, vegetation, or seaweed to form a symbol.
- In brush-covered areas, cut out patterns in the vegetation.
- In tundra, dig trenches or turn the soil upside down.
- In any terrain, use contrasting materials so that the symbols are visible to aircraft.

Reflector

On a sunny day, mirrors, polished canteen cups, belt buckles, or other objects will reflect the sun's rays.

Body signals

Receiver is operating

Affirmative (Yes)

Can proceed shortly, wait if possible

Do not attempt to land here

Pick us up, aircraft abandoned

Use drop message

Negative (No)

Land here (point in direction)

Body signals should be performed in an expansive, staccato fashion to deliver the following messages:

Need mechanical help or parts, long delay

All OK, do not wait

Need urgent medical help

Mirror signals can be seen for 62 miles (100km) under normal conditions and over 100 miles (160km) in a desert environment.

Ground-to-air signals

There are several factors you must take into account with regard to ground-to-air signals, if they are to be effective. Above all, visualize what your signal will look like when viewed by a pilot from the air. Therefore, signals should be as large as possible and in proper proportion. Make all pattern signals with straight lines and square corners (there are no straight lines or square corners in nature), and build them of materials that contrast with the background. On snow, for example, any dye used around the signal will add contrast. Note that orange material tends to blend in, not stand out, when placed on a green or brown background. Outline a signal with green boughs, brush, or rocks to produce shadows, or raise a panel on sticks to cast its own shadows. Your signal should be located where it can be seen from all directions (a large, open area is best).

The illustrations here show internationally recognized emergency signals. Learn them or, better still, carry a piece of paper around with you that lists them. When laying them out, make them as large as possible, at least 40 feet (10m) long and 10 feet (3m) wide. At night, dig or scrape a signal in the earth, snow, or sand, then pour in gasoline and ignite it. This signal will be visible not only at night, but also during the day where the ground has been burned.

Shadow signals can be effective for signaling, though you must construct them properly. Make sure you build them in a clearing, of a sufficient size, and that they contrast with their immediate surroundings. Follow these construction guidelines when making shadow signals in the following terrain:

Arctic winter: build a wall of snow blocks, and make sure you line them alongside the trench from which they were cut.

Arctic summer: construct walls from stones, sod, or wood.

Winter below the snow line: stick green boughs in the snow and build a wall of brush and boughs around them.

Summer below the tree line – use piles of rocks, dead wood, logs and blocks of sod cut out from the earth.

Destroy all ground-to-air symbols after rescue, or they will

Morse code

Morse code can be delivered via light or sound, and is internationally understood.

A .—	G ——.	M ——	S ...
B —...	H	N —.	T —
C —.—.	I ..	O ———	U ..—
D —..	J .———	P .——.	V ...—
E .	K —.—	Q ——.—	W .——
F ..—.	L .—..	R .—.	X —..—

go on marking after you have gone. Failure to do so may result in other aircraft spotting them and attempting a rescue. Information signals are used when you leave the scene of a crash or abandon camp—always leave a large arrow to indicate the direction in which you have set off.

Body signals

The illustration on pages 258–259 shows a series of body signals that will be understood by aircrew. It is advisable to use a cloth in the hand to emphasize the YES and NO signals. Note the changes from frontal to sideways positions and the use of the legs. Whenever you are making signals, always do so in a clear and exaggerated way.

An aircraft that has understood your message will tilt its wings up and down in daylight or make green flashes with its signal lights. If the pilot has not understood your message, he will circle his aircraft during daylight or make red flashes with his signals lights at night. Once a pilot has received and understood your first message, you can transmit other messages. Be patient: don't confuse the person flying the aircraft.

Mountain rescue codes

The codes listed below are internationally recognized mountain rescue signals. Learn them and practice transmitting them (you should always carry something to enable you to transmit a signal).

SOS—to send this signal use the following flare, sound, and light signals:
Flare: red.
Sound: three short blasts, three long blasts, three short blasts (repeat after a one-minute interval).
Light: three short flashes, three long flashes, three short flashes (repeat after a one-minute interval).

Help needed
Flare: red.
Sound: six blasts in quick succession (repeat after a one-minute interval).
Light: six flashes in quick succession (repeat after a one-minute interval).

Message understood
Flare: white.
Sound: three blasts in quick succession (repeat after a one-minute interval).
Light: three flashes in quick succession (repeat after a one-minute interval).

Return to base
Flare: green.
Sound: prolonged succession of blasts.
Light: prolonged succession of flashes.

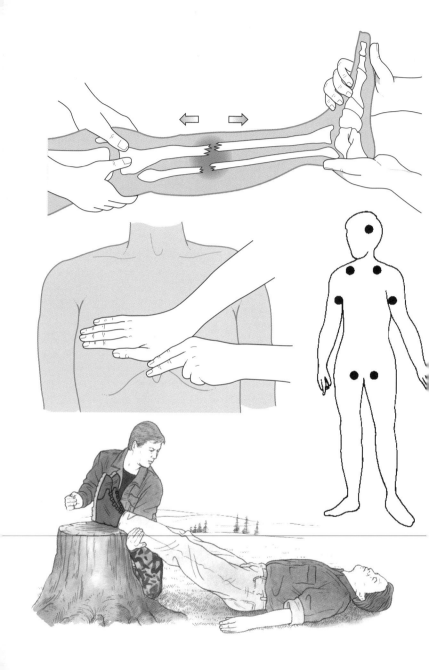

Wilderness first aid is not complicated, but you must have a thorough knowledge of it so that you can act decisively and quickly when the need arises. Speed is often the key to successful survival medicine.

PRIORITIES

In any accident situation, where there may be many injured people, always check for dangers to yourself before approaching victims. Beware of electric cables, fires, falling debris, dangerous structures, or wreckage. You should try to give a patient an initial checkup without moving him or her, but if there are dangers you will have to take a chance and move the patient and yourself to a safer location.

If the patient is breathing, ensure there is no obstruction in the mouth, and deal with any serious bleeding. Then place patient in the recovery position: if a patient is on his back, gently turn him or her on one side by grasping clothing at the hip. In this position, any liquids or vomit from the stomach or nose will not block the lungs, and the tongue will not fall back and block the airway.

....

Left: First aid incorporates a huge variety of techniques, though you should never lose sight of the three top priorities—ABC: Airway, Breathing, Circulation. Attend a professional first-aid course before your wilderness adventure.

9

First-aid decisions can quite literally make the difference between life and death.

First Aid

Recovery position

The recovery position involves placing the victim on his front, with one arm and one leg bent. Airways should be kept as free as possible. The position aids breathing and prevents victims from choking on their own vomit.

DO NOT, however, place a patient with a suspected spinal injury in the recovery position because you could cause permanent disability, even death.

Respiration/Maintaining Breathing

Every survivor must have a good knowledge of cardiopulmonary resuscitation (CPR), pulmonary resuscitation, and techniques for opening airways. The instant a person stops breathing and the heart stops beating, he or she is considered clinically dead. Within 4–6 minutes from that time, brain damage begins. Some 10 minutes after the heart has stopped, there is significant brain-cell death. This is called biological death and cannot be reversed. However, clinical death can be reversed in many cases. Breathing stops because of:

- Blockage of the upper air passages caused by face and neck injuries or foreign bodies.
- Choking.
- Inflammation and spasm of air passages caused by inhaling smoke, gases, or flame.
- Drowning or electrical shock.
- Compression of the chest.
- Lack of oxygen.

If a patient's breathing stops, you must take action to restart it. Begin artificial respiration at once.

SAS TIPS: PRIORITIES FOR TREATING PATIENTS

These are the priorities, as laid down by the British SAS, for dealing with injuries in an emergency situation. Do not deviate from this list. Knowing who to treat first can save lives. Prioritize treatment in the following order:

- Restore and maintain breathing and heartbeat.
- Stop bleeding.
- Protect wounds and burns.
- Immobilize fractures.
- Treat for shock.
- Remember: if a victim has multiple injuries, your treatment priorities for this patient are breathing, heartbeat, and bleeding.

Mouth-to-mouth resuscitation

Roll patient onto his or her back. Next, open the airway and check for breathing. You do this by using the head tilt: place the palm and fingers of your hand on the patient's forehead and apply firm, gentle backward pressure. This tilts the head backward and opens the mouth

Checking airways

To check if the injured person's airway is open, place your cheek near the patient's mouth to feel for breath on your face. At the same time, look down at the chest to see whether it is rising or falling. To open the airway, tilt the head gently backward by using two fingers held under the point of the chin.

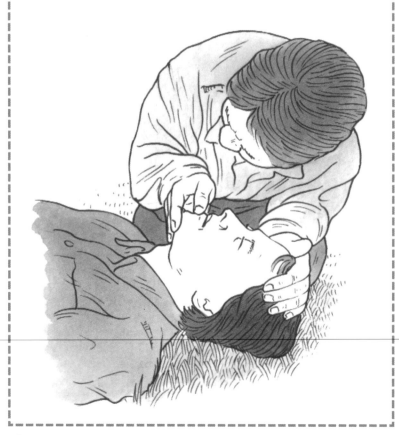

and hopefully the airway. Two other methods of opening the airway are to place one hand on the forehead and the fingers of the other under the chin, or to place one hand on the patient's forehead and the other under the neck.

These three methods may aggravate a spinal injury. Do not use them if you suspect a damaged spine. Instead, use the jaw thrust: rest your elbows on the ground and place one hand on each side of the patient's jaw. Following the contour of the jaw, push the jaw forward and apply most pressure with the index fingers: this will open the airway.

Next, clear any obstruction from the mouth or throat. Then place your ear near the patient's mouth to listen and feel for breathing, while also observing the chest for breathing movements. If a patient is not breathing, give four full breaths quickly by pinching the nose closed and blowing directly into the mouth (make sure your mouth makes a tight seal). These breaths should be quick enough to prevent the lungs from deflating between the next breath. Check that the chest falls automatically. Watch for the patient's chest to rise as you blow gently into his or her lungs. Deliver the first six inflations as quickly as possible, then at a rate of 12 per minute until breathing is established (be prepared for a long session, and don't give up). Never blow into the mouth of a

MOUTH-TO-NOSE RESUSCITATION

Use this method if you cannot give mouth-to-mouth resuscitation (if the patient has severe lacerations to the jaw, lips, or mouth, or if the jaws are clamped shut). Close and cover the patient's mouth with one hand and blow into the nose. Follow the same sequence as for mouth-to-mouth resuscitation.

person who is already breathing. If you cannot get any air into the lungs, the airway may be blocked. Remove any visible obstruction with your fingers. If you cannot see any obstruction, clear the airway by following the techniques as for choking (see below).

Cardiopulmonary resuscitation (CPR)
This is necessary if the patient's heart fails to function. In this case not only will you have to breathe for the person, but you will also have to perform chest compressions to force the heart to circulate the blood through the body. This action can restart the heart beat.

Cardiac massage

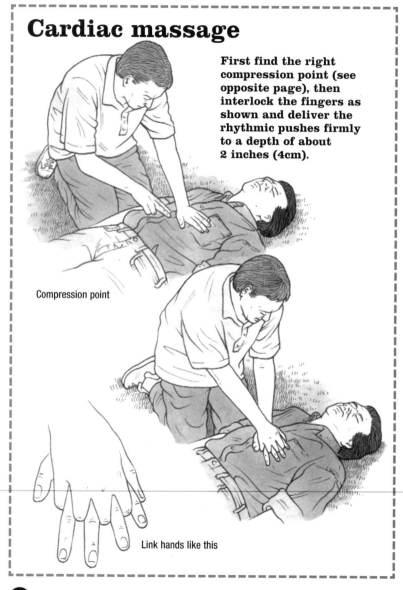

First find the right compression point (see opposite page), then interlock the fingers as shown and deliver the rhythmic pushes firmly to a depth of about 2 inches (4cm).

Compression point

Link hands like this

Locating the heart

To find the right compression point, trace the line of the ribs up to the sternum, then measure two finger widths above this point and place the heel of the hand here.

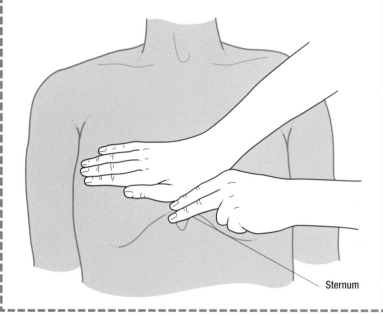

Sternum

Lie the patient on the ground, chest up. Trace the edge of his or her ribs with your index and middle fingers until you find the notch at the center of the lower chest where the ribs meet the bottom of the sternum. Keep your index finger on this spot and measure up two finger widths from the notch. Try to be as accurate as possible. Place the heel of your other hand just above and touching your fingers that are measuring up. The heel of your hand is now over the patient's heart. Be careful because you can damage the liver by giving compression too low on the chest.

Once the heel of your first hand is in position, place your other hand over it. You must kneel to perform CPR, with your shoulders directly

CANADIAN SPECIAL FORCES TIPS: SEQUENCE FOR CPR

Timely CPR can save a patient who would otherwise die. Learn the following Canadian Special Forces checklist for administering CPR.

- Check for consciousness.
- Establish and open airway.
- Look, listen, and feel for breathing.
- Give four rapid breaths.
- Check for pulse (while you look, listen, and feel for breaths).
- Locate the compression spot.
- Form proper hand position.
- Begin compressions: set of 15 compressions, then...
- Two quick breaths after each set of 15 compressions.
- After four complete sets of 15 compressions and two breaths, check for at least five seconds for pulse and breathing.

over the patient's sternum to push straight down on the heart. Compress the patient's chest 2 inches (4cm), with the movement being smooth, strong, and rhythmic, never jerky. Give CPR at a rate of 80 compressions a minute (100 for children, 100–120 for infants). It helps to count out loud, saying "one-and, two-and, three-and,..." Do not give up. Continue for at least an hour if necessary. Take turns if there is a group of you.

Two-person CPR

For two-person CPR, one person ventilates at the rate of one breath every five compressions. The second person gives compressions at the rate of 60 per minute, counting out loud "one-one thousand, two-one thousand, three-one thousand, four-one thousand, five-one thousand, one-one thousand," etc. Every one or two minutes, the person ventilating tells the compressor to stop for a pulse check. The ventilator checks for a pulse for a few compressions while the compressor is still giving compressions to ensure that the compressions are creating adequate circulation, then will say "Stop for pulse check," and will check for pulse and look and listen for any breathing.

If there is no pulse, the ventilator gives a full breath and says "continue compressions." If there is a pulse but no breathing, the ventilator says "we have a pulse" and continues

Finding a pulse

You can find a pulse at both the thumb-side edge of the wrist, and just beneath the angle of the jaw next to the windpipe. Use your fingers, not your thumb, to check for the pulse.

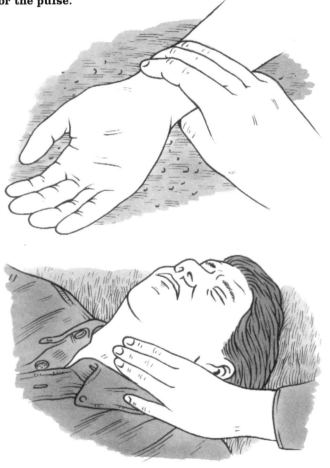

ventilating at one breath every five seconds. If there is a pulse and breathing, any other treatment the patient requires can now be given.

With a two-man CPR, you must be aware of the following:

- The person giving ventilations must time himself to the compressor's count.
- The ventilator should take in a deep breath on the count of four and blow into the patient exactly at the end of the fifth compression, just when the chest is beginning to rise.
- When changing places, the ventilator gives one more breath after the fifth compression and moves into position to begin compressions. Meanwhile, the second person begins a five-second pulse and breathing check. If there is no pulse or breathing, the ventilator gives a breath and the sequence then continues.

Choking

The following signs indicate that a person is choking:

- Patient is holding the throat.
- Inability to speak.
- Wheezing sounds and an effort in breathing.
- Inability to forcibly cough.
- Skin appears blue (in an unconscious patient).

Treating choking (1)

Firm slaps with heel of hand to the upper back

Self-treatment for choking—Heimlich maneuver

Choking responses begin with firmly delivered slaps on the back, and graduate to the Heimlich maneuver. Alternate between the techniques if neither is instantly successful.

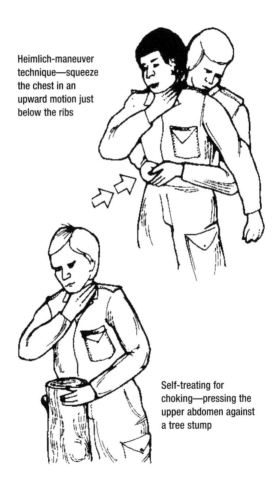

Heimlich-maneuver technique—squeeze the chest in an upward motion just below the ribs

Self-treating for choking—pressing the upper abdomen against a tree stump

• Chest not rising (in an unconscious patient).

In response, clear the airway with a finger and make sure the tongue has not fallen back and is obstructing the breathing passages. Then, administer four back blows with the heel of the hand, ensuring that the patient's head is lower than his chest. Strike the patient over the spine between the shoulder blades quickly and forcibly, but remember you are not trying to break his back. Be sensible.

If this fails to clear the blockage, try the Heimlich maneuver. Stand or kneel behind the patient with your arms around him. Clench one hand over the other, thumb-side of fist pressing between waist and bottom of ribs. Apply pressure and jerk quickly upward four times. If this fails, go back to four back blows. Repeat process until airway is clear or patient loses consciousness.

If the patient loses consciousness, lay him or her on his side and give four back blows. If this is unsuccessful, roll the patient on side and give four abdominal thrusts using the heel of your hand. After four thrusts, grab hold of the patient's lower jaw and tongue and pull the jaw out and upward to open the mouth. Sweep the mouth with your index finger, then tip the head into the CPR position (see above).

If there is no breathing, give four quick breaths. If lungs will not inflate,

Treating choking (2)

Technique for conscious person who is choking

A person who is choking can quickly lose consciousness if you don't act positively. If they are conscious, use a combination of the back-slapping and Heimlich techniques described in the main text. Should the choking victim lapse into unconsciousness, you can deliver a version of the Heimlich maneuver from a straddling position as shown.

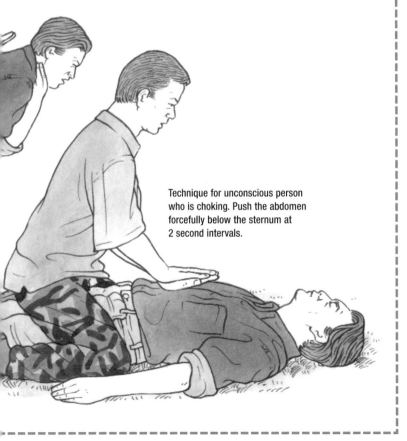

Technique for unconscious person who is choking. Push the abdomen forcefully below the sternum at 2 second intervals.

repeat sequence of four back blows, four abdominal thrusts, mouth sweep, check for breathing, and four quick breaths. If there is no pulse, begin CPR. If you are alone and are choking, give yourself abdominal thrusts with your hands or use a blunt projection such as a tree stump or branch.

Bleeding

When a patient is bleeding heavily, you must take immediate action to stop it. Apply pressure over the bleeding point (even minor arterial bleeding can be controlled with local pressure), and any bleeding extremities should be elevated above the heart. Use anything to stop the blood flow, but ensure it is clean. Maintain a firm, continuous pressure for 5–10 minutes, and when the bleeding has stopped use a dressing to keep the wound clean.

Tourniquets are a last-ditch option for use when severe bleeding cannot be controlled by any other method. You can place them only on the

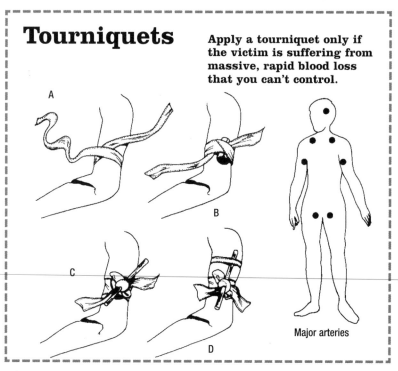

Tourniquets

Apply a tourniquet only if the victim is suffering from massive, rapid blood loss that you can't control.

A

B

C

D

Major arteries

Controlling blood loss

When treating an injured limb, maintain pressure on the bleeding wound with a clean pad and elevate the limb to a position higher than the victim's heart. This position reduces blood pressure in the limb, and therefore slows the bleeding.

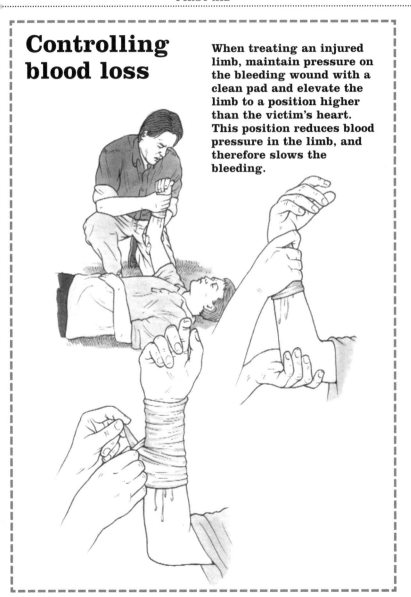

upper arm (just below the armpit) and around the upper thigh. Use a cloth at least 2 inches (5cm) wide. Wrap the cloth around the limb and tie a half knot. Place a stick over the knot and tie a double knot over it. Twist the stick to tighten the tourniquet until the bleeding stops.

Be warned: applying tourniquets can lead to the amputation of a limb, because tissue starts to die once it is cut off from the blood supply. For this reason, make sure that you release the tourniquet pressure every 10–15 minutes for one or two minutes' duration; this enables blood to flow back into the limb.

Internal bleeding presents different challenges. It results from a violent blow, broken bones, or deep wounds. Internal bleeding is indicated by faintness, light-headedness, pale skin that is cold and clammy to the touch, red-colored urine, blood passed with bowel motions, feces with a black, tarry appearance, vomiting blood, and coughing up blood. To treat, lie the victim flat on his or her back with their legs elevated. Keep them warm and hope for early rescue.

Shock
Shock is a condition caused by the critical reduction in the effective

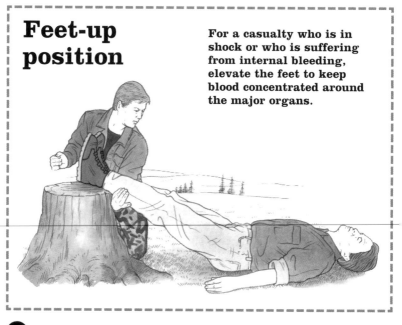

Feet-up position

For a casualty who is in shock or who is suffering from internal bleeding, elevate the feet to keep blood concentrated around the major organs.

U.S. ARMY TIPS: TREATMENT FOR SHOCK

Shock can be a killer. Follow the guidelines of the U.S. Army.
If conscious, place patient on a level surface with the lower extremities raised 6 to 8 inches (15 to 20cm).

- If unconscious, place patient on his or her side or abdomen with head turned to one side to prevent choking.
- Once patient is in shock position, do not move.
- Keep patient warm.
- If patient is wet, remove all wet clothing as quickly as possible and replace with dry items.
- Insulate patient from the ground with clothing, tree boughs, etc, and make a shelter to insulate him or her from the weather.
- Use hot liquids, food, or body heat to provide external warmth.
- Only administer liquids or foods if patient is conscious, and do not give if patient has abdominal wounds.
- Patient should rest for at least 24 hours.

volume of blood circulating in the patient's blood vessels. It can be the result of loss of blood through bleeding; loss of blood into the tissues, such as with a broken thigh; and loss of fluids through sweating, vomiting, and diarrhea. Shock is likely if a person has pale, cold, and clammy skin, a fast and weak pulse, and fast and shallow breathing.

To treat, ensure the airway is open. Any fractures should be treated and splinted (see pages 288–289). Keep the patient warm and still. Any rough handling of a patient suffering from shock is extremely dangerous. This sounds obvious, but in your efforts to treat a patient you may be too violent.

Wounds and dressings
Once bleeding has been stopped, you need to clean and dress any wound, particularly in a survival situation where an open wound will be dangerously exposed to dirt and disease. First irrigate the wound

SPECIAL FORCES TIPS: DEALING WITH WOUNDS

It is vital to prevent a wound from becoming infected. Special Forces manuals advise the following for the care of wounds in the wild:

- Clean a wound from the center outward.
  Change dressings if they become wet, omit offensive odors, or if the pain in the wound increases and throbs, indicating infection.
- Local infections can be treated with a poultice. Anything that can be mashed, such as rice, bark, or seeds, can be used. Boil and wrap in a cloth. Apply it to the infected area as hot as can be tolerated.
- A warm rock wrapped in cloth and applied to wound can aid healing.

Bandaging

Once a bleeding wound is under control, bandage a clean pad in place over the top of it. If blood starts to seep through, bandage another pad on top of the first to keep up the pressure.

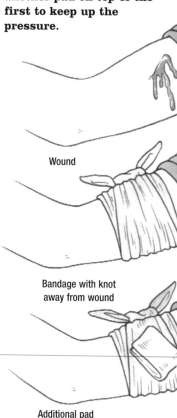

Wound

Bandage with knot away from wound

Additional pad

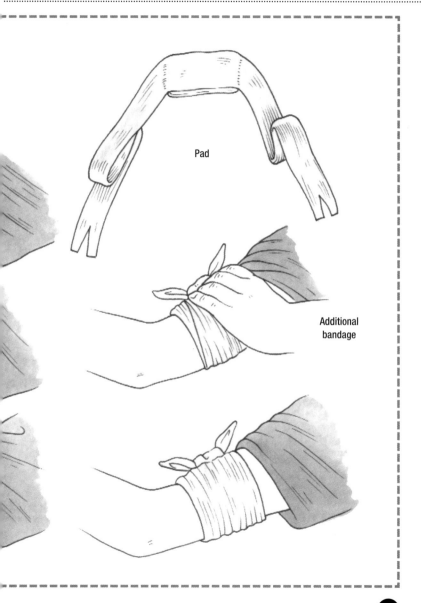

Pad

Additional bandage

Applying a roller bandage

Roller bandages are extremely easy to apply (A–C). Don't tie the bandage so tight that you cut off circulation to the limb. Pinch the casualty's nails (D) to see if the blood flows back into them when you release. It is doesn't, loosen the bandage.

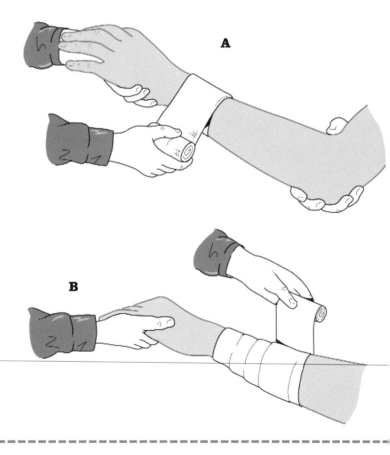

A

B

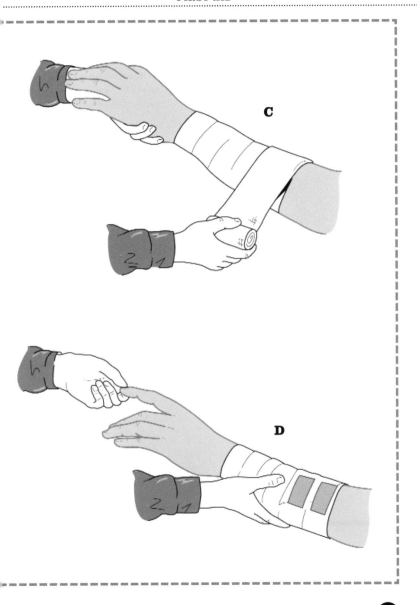

Stitching a wound

Stitching a wound is not recommended for those without professional medical training. If rescue will not arrive for a long time, however, it may be the only option.

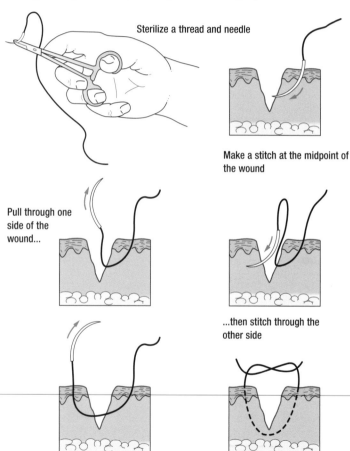

Sterilize a thread and needle

Make a stitch at the midpoint of the wound

Pull through one side of the wound...

...then stitch through the other side

Draw the wound together

Tie the stitch off. Repeat.

(wash by pouring or squirting, not scrubbing) with sterile saline solution or clean water. Close the wound (use butterfly bandages if available and the wound is not too deep). This is where your medical kit comes in handy, because you should coat the wound lightly with an antibiotic ointment and then apply a sterile dressing and bandage.

If, for any reason, a part of your body has been torn off, you must stop the bleeding and treat for shock. Irrigate and disinfect the area, apply antibiotic ointment and cover with a dressing. Place a sterile gauze pad over the dressing and bandage securely. Repeat this process each day, as well as scrub away all the yellowish crust and dead tissue (do this gently, as you don't want to reopen the wound).

Only attempt to suture a wound when it is deep and butterfly sutures will not work. You need one needle holder (forceps with a needle groove) and suture material. Suturing is simply stitching. When you are stitching each stitch you should go to the bottom of the wound to prevent pockets or air and blood forming and to take in equal amounts of tissue on both sides of the wound to align the edges. To secure sutures, tie them off with a square knot (see Chapter 6). Leave the sutures in for 10 days and then remove with fine scissors. Grasp the knot with forceps and tweezers and pull stitch out with a firm tug.

DRESSINGS AND HYGIENE

Dressings act as poison collectors, so do not reuse them. In a survival situation, where you may be using strips of clothing for dressings, you will have to reuse them. Wash them thoroughly and boil for at least 15 minutes.

BREAKS AND FRACTURES

A fracture is a chip, crack, or break of a bone. There are two types of fracture: open and closed. In an open fracture, the bone has come through the skin or something has penetrated the skin and broken the bone. With a closed fracture, the bone is broken but there is no opening of the skin.

Closed fracture

If you suspect a closed fracture, check for a pulse at the wrist. If circulation is impeded (the hands feel cold and lacking sensation or there is no pulse), you must restore the flow of blood to the lower arm at once, otherwise the limb will have to be amputated. Apply traction (a continuous pull) and try to restore pulse and nerve response. Don't

U.S. ARMY SPECIAL FORCES TIPS: LIST OF SYMPTOMS TO IDENTIFY FRACTURES

The Green Berets are experts in survival medicine. Use their training and learn to identify the symptoms that can indicate a fractured limb.

- Patient feels or hears the bone break.
- Partial or complete loss of motion.
- Grating sound when limbs are moved.
- Deformity and abnormal motion at fracture site, such as arm bending but not at the elbow.
- Tenderness around the injury.
- Muscle spasm.

Broken limb

Broken limbs can be either closed fractures, in which case the injury has not broken the skin, or open fractures, where the sharp end of the broken bone has torn through the skin. The latter needs to be treated both as a fracture injury and as a bleeding injury.

Normal

Closed fracture

Open fracture

worry if you have only partial nerve response. You will have to wait until you get back to civilization for complete restoration (full nerve response can often be restored by surgical techniques—reassure the patient of this).

Now release the traction slowly, while still checking for pulse and nerve response. If these remain, splint the injured limb securely (immobilize the joint on either side of the fracture).

Open fracture

For an open fracture, first control the bleeding if it is severe (see wounds and dressings). Check for nerve

Aligning a broken leg

In the case of a fracture, traction is the process of aligning the bones so that normal blood flow to the limb is resumed. Draw the extremity toward you with a slow, firm pressure, taking your time so that the casualty can relax his leg muscles.

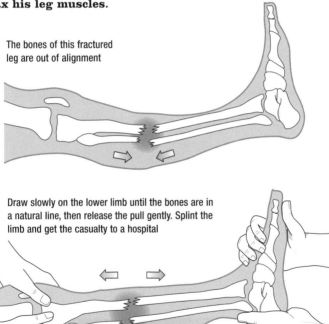

The bones of this fractured leg are out of alignment

Draw slowly on the lower limb until the bones are in a natural line, then release the pull gently. Splint the limb and get the casualty to a hospital

response, then irrigate the wound, removing any bone chips or foreign bodies. Apply traction and try to reset the fracture and close the wound (do it slowly). After traction, inspect the wound to ensure the bone ends align properly. Then splint, but in a way that lets you work on the wound.

Splinting an arm and leg

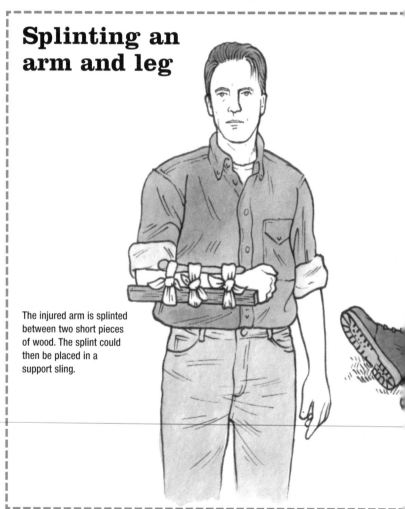

The injured arm is splinted between two short pieces of wood. The splint could then be placed in a support sling.

(Always check for pulse and nerve response; if there aren't any, you must repeat resetting and traction procedures).

Spinal injuries

Any injury to the spinal column can cause paralysis and is potentially fatal. Signs of spinal injury are: pain

Splinting is the process of immobilizing a fractured or dislocated limb so that it suffers no further injury during subsequent movement. Branches will provide basic splints, but you can also improvise them out of walking poles, rolled-up newspapers and magazines, or tent pegs.

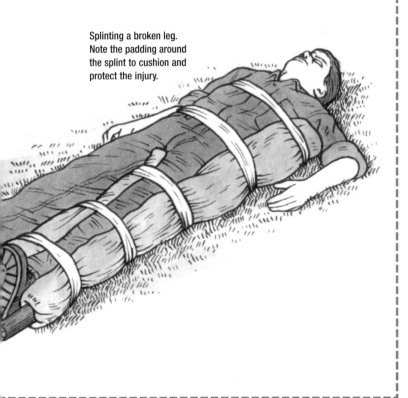

Splinting a broken leg. Note the padding around the splint to cushion and protect the injury.

Stabilizing the neck

If someone has suffered a neck injury, it is imperative that they do not move (unless there is greater danger in not doing so) and that the head and neck are stabilized in a natural position.

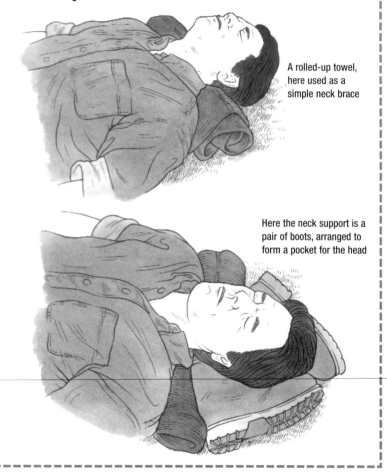

A rolled-up towel, here used as a simple neck brace

Here the neck support is a pair of boots, arranged to form a pocket for the head in the back without movement; deformity in the spinal column; any spot along the spinal column tender to the touch; persistent erection of the penis; arms uncontrollably extended above the head; loss of bladder control.

Always be careful when attempting to move a patient with a spinal injury. If patient is face-up, place a folded blanket under the small of the back to stop bone fragments from lacerating or compressing the spinal column. If patient is face-down, place a folded blanket under the chest. When moving the patient, always treat the entire spinal column as a nonflexible unit—use a rigid litter or board longer than the patient is tall for transportation.

Fractured ribs

For fracture of the upper ribs, have the patient hold his or her breath while you apply two long adhesive strips across the shoulder of the injured side. For fracture of the lower ribs, apply a piece of felt or foam rubber over the fracture. Have the patient hold his or her breath while you apply adhesive strips around the injured side of the trunk. Another method for treating fractures of both the upper and lower ribs is to apply an elastic bandage around the trunk of the body from below the costal cage to just below the level of the nipples. Whatever treatment you use, the fracture will take 4–6 weeks to heal. Fractured ribs can be painful; it is therefore important for the patient to get as much rest as possible.

SMALL BREAKS

In a survival situation, it is usually toes and fingers that are broken. A finger should be reset and splinted with wood or similar material. Broken toes should be reset and taped to an unbroken toe next to it.

NECK FRACTURE

To stabilize a neck fracture, immobilize the patient's neck with a cervical collar, or place a small rolled-up towel or sheet under the neck and place sandbags or boots filled with dirt or sand on either side of the head to control it. Keep the victim completely still and hope for speedy rescue.

Making a makeshift crutch

Invest in making improvised crutches only if the casualty will have to move himself to get to safety, and cannot do so unaided. The branch should be about the length from the armpit to the ground.

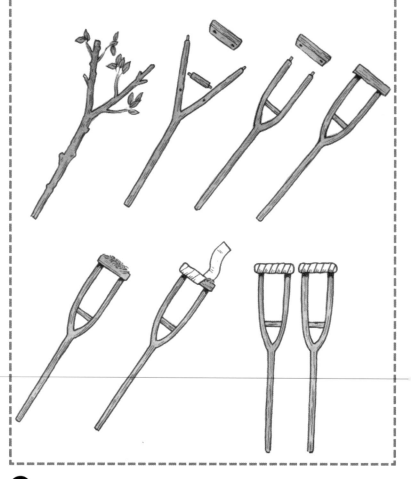

Skull fracture

Indications of a fractured skull can be straw-colored fluid seeping from the ear or nose. Place the casualty in the recovery position, leaking side down. Allow the fluid to escape, completely immobilize the patient, and keep him comfortable until you can get medical help.

STRAINS, SPRAINS, AND DISLOCATIONS

Sprains, strains, and dislocations can be common in a survival situation. A strain is a tearing or overstretching of a muscle. A sprain is a wrenching or tearing of tissues connected with the joint. A dislocation, usually caused by a fall, blow, or sudden force applied to a joint, forces the joint out of place.

For strains and sprains, rest the limb and apply cold packs to ease the pain. Apply these packs to the area straight after injury to reduce the swelling and pain, and immobilize the injury and treat like a fracture. Over several days or even weeks, reintroduce movement until the injured joint returns to full flexibility.

Dislocations

When dislocations occur, swelling will begin and the injury will be acutely painful. The joint must be reset before the swelling and muscle spasms make resetting difficult (the muscles near the joint will start to tighten up almost immediately). If you

SAS TIPS: TREATMENT FOR SPRAINS

SAS soldiers fight on foot most of the time, and can suffer sprained ankles. They therefore have to have effective treatments for sprains:

- Bathe sprain with cold water to reduce swelling.
- Support with bandage: do not constrict circulation.
- Elevate affected limb and rest completely.
- After spraining an ankle, keep your boot on if you keep walking—the boot will act as a splint. If you take it off, the swelling will prevent you from putting it back on again.

fail to do this, you risk the patient succumbing to gangrene or getting a permanent deformity.

To reset, apply traction to the joint and then move the extremity attached to it in the direction that it would normally move. This should realign the joint and take pressure off blood vessels and nerves. Release traction slowly to move the joint back into place and check for nerve

R.I.C.E.

The RICE acronym is a simple way to remember how to treat swelling injuries: Rest, Ice, Compression, Elevation.

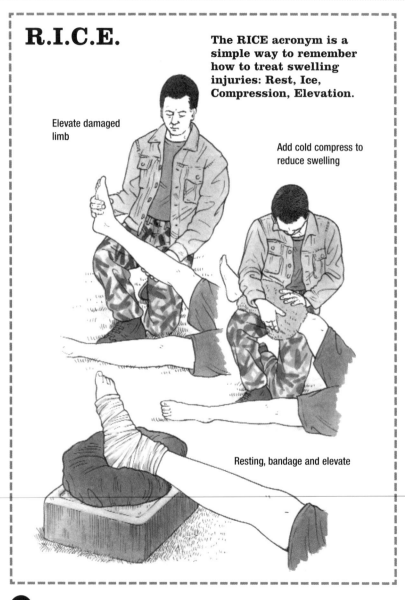

Elevate damaged limb

Add cold compress to reduce swelling

Resting, bandage and elevate

Support sling

To make a support
sling for a damaged
elbow, wind a large
sheet around the back
of the neck, and down
around the injured
limb (A), then back up
to tie at the neck (B).
An additional
bandage around the
torso (C) will help
keep the injury stable
during transit.

A

B

C

TREATMENT FOR POISONING

Special forces soldiers have fought in the exotic regions of the world for more than 50 years, and they have well-tested rules for dealing with poisoning.

- With suspected plant poisoning, induce vomiting.
- Alternatively, make an antidote: mix tea and charcoal with an equal part of milk of magnesia if available. The charcoal absorbs the poison and carries it from the body.
- Wash poisoned skin with soap and water and remove contaminated clothing.
- Sluice chemical poisons off the skin with water (though try to ascertain the properties of the chemicals to which you have been exposed).
- With inhaled poisons, move the patient to fresh air, loosen tight clothing, and give artificial respiration.

response. If there is a pinched nerve, repeat the procedure. Application of cold packs will help reduce pain and swelling. Rest the extremity until fully healed.

POISONING

The main kinds of poisoning a survivor will face are eating dangerous plants, animals, and marine life and being bitten or stung. To treat a bite from a scorpion or spider, clean the wound and try to remove the poison by a suction device or by squeezing the bite site (though this may prove fruitless). If you have tobacco, chew it and place it over the bite site to ease the pain. Treat the bite as for an open wound, and hopefully the patient will ride out the poisoning symptoms (though your priority should be to get him to a hospital).

Snakebites

The symptoms of snakebite vary according the the type of snake, but can include tissue swelling at the bite site, gradually spreading to surrounding area; blood in the urine; severe headaches and thirst; irregular heartbeat; weakness and exhaustion; dizziness; blurred vision; confusion; lack of muscular coordination and twitching; respiratory difficulty; tingling; excessive perspiration, numbness of the lips and soles of the feet; nausea; vomiting and diarrhea; unconsciousness; and a drop in

Snakebite

A bite mark from a poisonous snake is generally indicated by two large puncture holes at the front of the bite, made by the venom-injecting fangs.

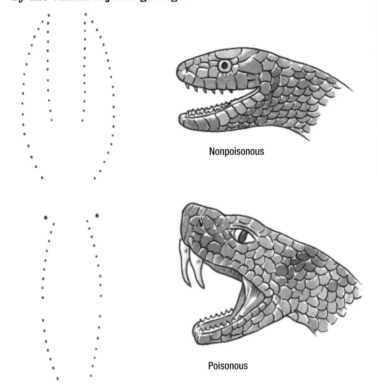

Nonpoisonous

Poisonous

blood pressure and a corresponding rise of pulse rate. Death can occur within 24–48 hours if the bite is serious and untreated, and there is a real danger of a loss of limbs.

All snakebite victims will need treatment for shock. If no antivenom is available, place a restricting bandage, NOT A TOURNIQUET, above the bite and bandage down

Cleaning a bite

Irrigate a bite by pouring clean water over it. Direct the water so that it flows quickly off the body—it could be carrying the bite toxins.

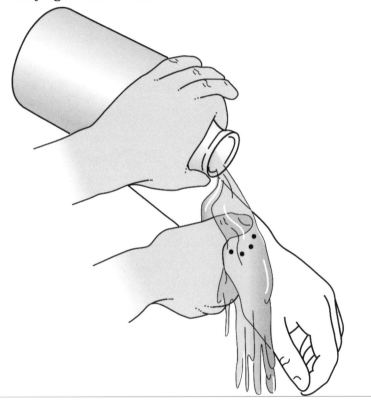

over the site. Use cool water or ice to keep as cool as possible. Get the patient to professional medical help as your absolute priority.

BURNS

Burns can be life-threatening in a survival situation in the wilderness. There are three types:

- First degree, which usually involve the first layer of skin. These are not serious.
- Second degree, which involve the second layer of skin. These burns are very red, produce blisters, and are intensely painful for up to 48 hours. There is fluid loss and a danger of infection.
- Third degree, which destroy the first two layers of skin and damages deeper tissues. There is severe fluid loss and a danger of infection. The burned area is usually charred black, and the victim will suffer great pain.

With any burn, the first response should be to cool it—the heat of a burn continues to damage tissue long after the initial accident. Pour cooling water continually over the injury (or immerse the injured body part in cold water), or apply cold compresses, refreshing them with cold water when they become warm. Keep doing this for approximately 10 minutes, then remove all foreign matter from the injury. Next, cover the injury with a nonadhering sterile gauze pad. Do not use an airtight dressing. Remove the dressing every day and scrub the wound with a

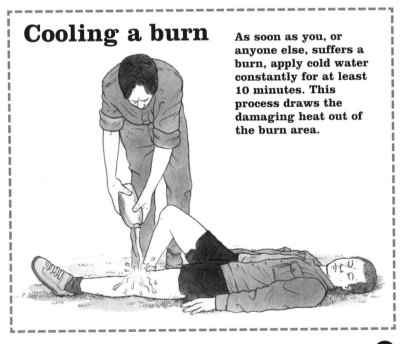

Cooling a burn

As soon as you, or anyone else, suffers a burn, apply cold water constantly for at least 10 minutes. This process draws the damaging heat out of the burn area.

sterile gauze pad and peroxide (if you have it). All white and yellow dead tissue must be removed every day. The patient also has to replace fluids orally. Make him drink lots of water but keep an eye on his urine flow. Cut down the amount of water if it becomes very high. Be prepared to treat him for shock.

COLD-RELATED INJURIES

Cold-weather climates can produce a host of injuries in the unwary. A suprisingly common condition is dehydration, more often associated with hot climates. The first indication that you are dehydrated is the color of your urine, which will appear dark yellow. Other symptoms are no appetite, moving in slow motion, drowsiness, and a higher than normal temperature. In cold weather, you must drink plenty of liquids, such as water, tea, or soup to avoid dehydration. Avoid alcohol. It can dull your mind and lead to frostbite.

Hypothermia

Hypothermia is the real killer in cold climates. It involves the cooling of the body below its normal temperature of 97–100°F (36–38°C), and is potentially life-threatening. The symptoms are (in order): mild shivering; uncontrollable shivering (you will have difficulty controlling your fingers and hands); violent shivering (difficulty speaking); shivering slows down and stops; irrationality; inability to make decisions; unconsciousness and then death. Keep watch for any signs of shivering. Be extra alert for when the shivering slows down or stops. This is a critical warning.

The treatment for hypothermia is heat. Stop what you are doing and get out of the cold. Build a fire, get dry, drink warm fluids, eat chocolate. Do NOT drink alcohol because it will only result in the loss of core heat. If you come across a person who is hypothermic, get him out of the wind and into shelter. Remove wet clothing and replace with dry items. Place warm rocks (wrapped in cloth to prevent burns) or water bottles filled with warm water near the patient's throat, armpits, and groin. Build a fire to provide heat. You may have to perform CPR.

Trench foot

Trench foot is an injury caused by exposure to the cold and wet. In the early stages, the feet and toes appear pale and feel numb, cold, and stiff. The victim finds walking and difficult and their feet swell and become painful. You must be alert to prevent development of trench foot because it can lead to limb amputation. To prevent trench foot, make sure you clean and dry your socks and boots regularly, and dry your feet as quickly as possible if they get wet. If you are wearing wet boots and socks, exercise your feet continually by wriggling your toes and bending your ankles.

When treating trench foot, handle the feet very gently. Do not walk if you have trench foot, and do not rub or massage your feet. Clean carefully with soap and water, dry, and then elevate.

Frostbite

Frostbite is extremely serious, leading to the loss of toes, fingers, arms, legs, and life. Factors that lead to frostbite include inadequate clothing, fatigue, too much alcohol, and restricted circulation, all in the context to exposure subzero temperatures.

Superficial frostbite strikes the fingers, hands, toes, feet, and face, and sometimes knees and upper legs. The skin appears white, waxy, and firm. The area will be numb, and may have a blue or purple outline. Deep frostbite is a complete freezing of a part of the body. The affected area will be white and hard and completely numb.

To treat frostbite: NEVER thaw an area if there is a chance of refreezing.

PREVENTING FROSTBITE

Special forces soldiers often go on exercises in the Arctic. They know that frostbite is a dangerous enemy, and they take every precaution to prevent it.

- Wrinkle your face to stop stiff patches from forming, and exercise the hands.
- Keep an eye on yourself and others for patches of white, waxy skin, especially on the face, ears, and hands.
- Do not wear tight clothing because it will restrict circulation.
- Dress inside your sleeping bag.
- Always wear the proper clothing outdoors. If it gets wet, dry it out as quickly as possible.
- Brush all snow off clothing before entering shelter, otherwise it will melt and wet the clothing.
- Keep your hands dry. Wear gloves and don't touch metal with bare hands. If you do, you will suffer cold burns.
- Be extra careful if you are very tired and rest if you are sick.

When you are in a safe location, you can thaw the affected parts by gently soaking them in water that is kept at a temperature of 100–110°F (38–43°C)—it feels warm to the touch. The flesh should turn to pink or red: at this point, you will experience extreme pain. Large blisters will form in a day: DO NOT lance them—they will break in 2 to 3 weeks. When they do break, treat the area as you would a burn.

With deep frostbite, a hard black shell will form over the area. Leave it: it is protecting damaged tissue and will come off on its own in 3 to 6 weeks. The area should heal totally within six months to a year. Remember: do not thaw slowly in cold water; do not thaw by holding close to a fire; do not rub the area, especially with snow.

Snow blindness

To prevent snowblindess, wear sunglasses. If you do go snow blind, your eyes will be red and sore; they will water and you will have a headache. Treatment includes blindfolding yourself and waiting until the soreness disappears. If you don't have sunglasses, improvise a pair from cardboard or tree bark, with thin slits for the eyes.

HEAT-RELATED INJURIES

Heat-related injuries result from a deficiency of salt or water during heavy sweating, apart from heatstroke, which results from a failure of the body's sweating mechanisms.

Heat cramps are caused by excessive loss of salt from the body

Treating heat exhaustion

When someone is suffering from heat exhaustion, the first response is to get them rested in the shade, with their feet elevated and clothes loosened. Give him or her frequent sips of water to rehydrate.

when you have been sweating heavily. The cramps are painful spasms of the muscles, usually legs, arms, and abdominals, and can be mild or severe. Treat by drinking large amounts of water.

Heat exhaustion is caused by excessive loss of water and salt from the body through sweating. The skin becomes cold and wet with sweat, with accompanying headache, dizziness, weakness, and loss of

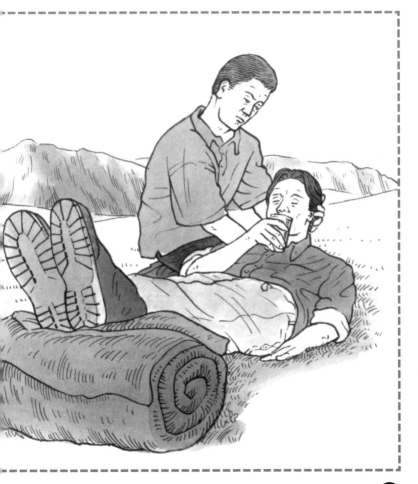

appetite. The condition can be fatal if untreated. Place the victim in the shade. Massage and elevate the legs to return blood to the heart. Give him large quantities of water to drink.

Heatstroke occurs when the body loses its ability to cool itself by sweating. The skin becomes hot and dry, and the victim may suddenly collapse or experience

Water blanket treatment

headache, dizziness, or even delirium before becoming unconscious. Heatstroke is potentially fatal. The treatment is aimed at lowering the body

For those in a critical state of heatstroke (hyperthermia), one method of treatment is to wrap them in a sheet or blanket and soak the material with cold water. The cold sheet draws heat out of the casualty's body. Keep the sheet refreshed with cold water, and fan it to increase heat loss through evaporation.

U.S. MARINE CORPS TIPS: TREATMENT FOR ALL HEAT INJURIES

Desert heat injuries can be potentially fatal. You must administer treatment immediately. Follow these U.S. Marine Corps guidelines:

- Your primary aim is to lower the patient's body temperature immediately.
- Place the patient on his or her back in a shady place.
- Loosen their clothing.
- Sprinkle the patient with water.
- Fan the patient.
- If the patient is conscious and rational, give him or her a salt tablet and plenty of cool (not cold) water to drink.
- Do not administer any stimulants.

temperature as quickly as possible. Place the patient in the shade, remove clothing, and sprinkle his body with water from head to foot. Fan to increase the cooling effect. Massage the legs and arms to stimulate circulation.

GLOSSARY OF SURVIVAL TERMS

bearing—the compass direction from your position to a landmark or destination.

bola—a weapon consisting of multiple weights bound together by rope and thrown to bring down prey.

calorie—the amount of heat required to raise the temperature of 1 gram of water by 1°Celsius.

carbohydrate—an organic compound of carbon, hydrogen, and oxygen found in many foods. When ingested, carbohydrates are broken down to provide energy.

chart—a map used for navigation at sea or in an aircraft.

chlorine—a chemical element that may be added to water as a purifying agent.

coniferous—denotes an evergreen tree with cones and needlelike leaves.

contour—a line on a map joining points of equal elevation.

coordinates—a pair of numbers and/or letters that describe a unique position

course—the route or path between two points.

cyclone—a large-scale, atmospheric wind-and-pressure system characterized by low pressure at its center and by circular wind motion, counterclockwise in the Northern Hemisphere, clockwise in the Southern Hemisphere.

datum—a reference point used by cartographers, from which all elevations or positions on a map or chart are measured.

deadfall trap—a trap designed to kill an animal by dropping a heavy weight on it.

degree (or °)—the unit of measurement of an angle. A full circle is divided into 360°; each degree is divided into 60 minutes, and each minute into 60 seconds.

dehydration—in a person, a significant loss of body fluids that are not replaced by fluid intake.

dysentery—a chronic diarrheal illness that can lead to severe dehydration and, ultimately, death.

elevation—height above mean sea level.

fats—natural oily substances which, in humans, are derived from food and deposited in subcutaneous layers and around some major organs.

grid—the horizontal and vertical lines on a map that enable you to describe position.

grid reference—a position defined in relation to a cartographic grid.

hyperthermia—a condition in which the body temperature rises to a dangerously high level. Also known as heatstroke.

hypothermia—a condition in which the body temperature falls to a dangerously low level. Also known as exposure.

iodine—a chemical element that has a use in water purification.

kindling—small pieces of dry material, usually thin twigs, added to ignited tinder to develop a fire.

latitude—a measure of distance north or south of the equator.

longitude—a measure of distance east or west of the prime meridian.

lure—anything used in fishing or hunting that tempts prey into a trap or particular location.

magnetic north—the direction of the magnetic north pole.

mammals—warm-blooded vertebrates that usually give birth to live young.

minerals—inorganic substances that the human body requires to maintain health.

monsoon—a period of intense rainfall and wind in India and Southeast Asia between May and September annually.

nautical mile—the standard measurement of distance used by marine navigators. It is equal to one minute of longitude, or 1.852km or 1.151 imperial miles.

potassium permanganate—a chemical that can be used to sterilize water.

proteins—organic compounds that form an essential part of living organisms. Among other things, they are integral to the function of body tissue, muscle, and antibodies.

quarry—in tracking, the animal or human that is being hunted or pursued.

satellite geometry—the arrangement of satellites in the sky above a GPS receiver as it tries to compute its position.

savannah—grassy plains of tropical and subtropical regions with flat terrain and very few trees.

solar still—a device that traps moisture from the soil under a plastic sheet, this condensing out into drinkable water.

stalking—in tracking, the art of moving silently and stealthily so as not to alert the quarry to your presence.

temperate—any climate characterized by mild temperatures.

tinder—small pieces of light and dry material that are very easily ignited and are used to initiate a fire.

track—a line of sign that indicates the route of an animal or human quarry through the environment.

tracking—the pursuit of an animal or human quarry by observing and following the sign they have left behind. See also sign.

trailing—another word for tracking.

transit—an imaginary straight line extended through two landmarks and used as a position line.

transpiration bag—a plastic bag tied around vegetation to trap water vapor emitted by the plant and condense it out into drinking water.

tropical—denotes the latitudes 23° 26′ north or south of the equator.

true north—the direction of the geographic north pole.

vitamins—a group of organic compounds that are an essential part of human nutrition, though they are required in only very small doses.

Index